most loved recipe collection most loved recipe collection most loved recipe collection

most
loved

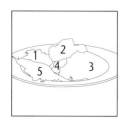

Pictured on front cover:
1. Wild Rice Stuffing, page 57
2. Marmalade-Glazed Sweet Potatoes, page 74
3. Roast Turkey, page 52
4. Cranberry Sauce, page 55
5. Confetti Beans, page 78

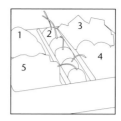

Pictured on back cover:
1. Rum Balls, page 112
2. Chocolate Cherries, page 110
3. Old-Fashioned Toffee, page 108
4. Pecan Balls, page 110
5. Five-Minute Fudge, page 108

Most Loved Holiday Favourites
Copyright © Company's Coming Publishing Limited

First Printing November 2007

Library and Archives Canada Cataloguing in Publication
Paré, Jean, date
Most loved holiday favourites / Jean Paré.
(Most loved recipe collection)
Includes index.
ISBN 978-1-897069-17-2
1. Christmas cookery. I. Title. II. Series: Paré, Jean, date-.
Most loved recipe collection
TX739.2.C45P384 2007   641.5'686   C2007-901718-5

Published by
Company's Coming Publishing Limited
2311 – 96 Street
Edmonton, Alberta, Canada T6N 1G3
Tel: 780-450-6223   Fax: 780-450-1857
www.companyscoming.com

Company's Coming is a registered trademark owned by
Company's Coming Publishing Limited

We acknowledge the financial support of the Government of Canada through the Book Publishing Industry Development Program (BPIDP) for our publishing activities.

Printed in China

We gratefully acknowledge the following suppliers for their generous support of our Test and Photography Kitchens:

Broil King Barbecues
Corelle®
Hamilton Beach® Canada
Lagostina®
Proctor Silex® Canada
Tupperware®

Our special thanks to the following businesses for providing props for photography:

Call the Kettle Black
Casa Bugatti
Cherison Enterprises Inc.
Chintz & Company
Danesco Inc.
Dansk Gifts
La Cache
Le Gnome
Linens 'N Things
Michael's the Arts and Crafts Store
Mikasa Home Store
Pier 1 Imports
Sears Canada
Stokes
Totally Bamboo
The Bay
When Pigs Fly
Winners Stores
Zellers
Zenari's

Pictured from left: Peppermint Nanaimo Bars, page 100; Scallop Attraction, page 40; Stuffing Balls, page 56; Chocolate Roulade Yule Log, page 88

table of contents

"never share a recipe you wouldn't use yourself"

the Company's Coming story

Jean Paré (pronounced "jeen PAIR-ee") grew up understanding that the combination of family, friends and home cooking is the best recipe for a good life. From her mother, she learned to appreciate good cooking, while her father praised even her earliest attempts in the kitchen. When Jean left home, she took with her a love of cooking, many family recipes and an intriguing desire to read cookbooks as if they were novels!

In 1963, when her four children had all reached school age, Jean volunteered to cater the 50th Anniversary of the Vermilion School of Agriculture, now Lakeland College, in Alberta, Canada. Working out of her home, Jean prepared a dinner for more than 1,000 people, which launched a flourishing catering operation that continued for over 18 years. During that time, she had countless opportunities to test new ideas with immediate feedback— resulting in empty plates and contented customers! Whether preparing cocktail sandwiches for a house party or serving a hot meal for 1,500 people, Jean Paré earned a reputation for good food, courteous service and reasonable prices.

As requests for her recipes mounted, Jean was often asked the question, "Why don't you write a cookbook?" Jean responded by teaming up with her son, Grant Lovig, in the fall of 1980 to form Company's Coming Publishing Limited. The publication of *150 Delicious Squares* on April 14, 1981 marked the debut of what would soon become one of the world's most popular cookbook series.

The company has grown since those early days when Jean worked from a spare bedroom in her home. Today, she continues to write recipes while working closely with the staff of the Recipe Factory, as the Company's Coming test kitchen is affectionately known. There she fills the role of mentor, assisting with the development of recipes people most want to use for everyday cooking and easy entertaining. Every Company's Coming recipe is *kitchen-tested* before it's approved for publication.

Jean's daughter, Gail Lovig, is responsible for marketing and distribution, leading a team that includes sales personnel located in major cities across Canada. In addition, Company's Coming cookbooks are published and distributed under licence in the United States, Australia and other world markets. Bestsellers many times over in English, Company's Coming cookbooks have also been published in French and Spanish.

Familiar and trusted in home kitchens around the world, Company's Coming cookbooks are offered in a variety of formats. Highly regarded as kitchen workbooks, the softcover Original Series, with its lay-flat plastic comb binding, is still a favourite among readers.

Jean Paré's approach to cooking has always called for *quick and easy recipes* using *everyday ingredients.* That view has served her well. The recipient of many awards, including the Queen Elizabeth Golden Jubilee medal, Jean was appointed a Member of the Order of Canada, her country's highest lifetime achievement honour.

Jean continues to gain new supporters by adhering to what she calls The Golden Rule of Cooking: *"Never share a recipe you wouldn't use yourself."* It's an approach that works— *millions of times over!*

foreword

Come the middle of November, calendars seem to sprout ink. Every time you turn around, another square's filled in! There's the neighbourhood skating party, the school concert (with the notation to bring some baking for the bake sale), your aunt's annual potluck and your girlfriends' gift exchange—just to name a few. And at each of these joyful, special occasions, the food that is shared is spiced with the traditions of the season.

At Company's Coming, we know how important it is to be able to rely on delicious, fail-safe recipes during these busy weeks. That's why we've collected our favourites from cookbooks past to create *Most Loved Holiday Favourites*, a treasury of Christmas delights.

Let's start with the sweets—such a nice place to start! Our fudge, toffee, bark and brittle, for instance, not only dress up any dessert tray, but they also make wonderful handmade gifts. And if you're looking for the perfect gingerbread recipe to while away a cozy afternoon with little ones, it's tucked into our sweets & treats section, along with even more goodies for parties and cookie exchanges.

But it's not all about visions of sugar plums. You'll find essential appetizers for the tree trimming or cocktail gathering, mulled wine to warm up carollers and a tourtière to serve on Christmas Eve. As for the feast itself, we offer the standard roast turkey as well as ham, pork loin and beef. (The Grinch would be happy to carve any of these roast beasts!)

To make your life easier, we've added sidebars with make-ahead instructions, as well as handy tips on everything from candy thermometers to gift giving. We've also sprinkled *Most Loved Holiday Favourites* with interesting holiday trivia— do *you* know why traditional nutcrackers have bared teeth, or how Boxing Day came to be?

This Christmas season, let us help you create happy, stress-free memories with our collection of festive favourites. It's our gift to you, along with our wishes for a warm, happy holiday.

Jean Paré

nutrition information

Each recipe is analyzed using the most current version of the Canadian Nutrient File from Health Canada, which is based on the United States Department of Agriculture (USDA) Nutrient Database.

- If more than one ingredient is listed (such as "butter or hard margarine"), or if a range is given (1 – 2 tsp., 5 – 10 mL), only the first ingredient or first amount is analyzed.

- For meat, poultry and fish, the serving size per person is based on the recommended 4 oz. (113 g) uncooked weight (without bone), which is 2 – 3 oz. (57 – 85 g) cooked weight (without bone)—approximately the size of a deck of playing cards.

- Milk used is 1% M.F. (milk fat), unless otherwise stated.

- Cooking oil used is canola oil, unless otherwise stated.

- Ingredients indicating "sprinkle," "optional," or "for garnish" are not included in the nutrition information.

- The fat in recipes and combination foods can vary greatly depending on the sources and types of fats used in each specific ingredient. For these reasons, the amount of saturated, monounsaturated and polyunsaturated fats may not add up to the total fat content.

Vera C. Mazurak, Ph.D.
Nutritionist

These versatile muffins make for great breakfast fare, but also work for luncheons, snacks and afternoon teas. Keep plenty on hand for all your holiday visitors.

christmas fun

So what exactly are the twelve days of Christmas? In the western world, the twelve days start on Christmas and end on January sixth. In Christian religions, this time span is meant to represent the time between the birth of Jesus and the Epiphany, a day marked by the visit of the three Magi bearing their gifts for the baby.

Raspberry Cream Muffins

All-purpose flour	2 cups	500 mL
Baking powder	1 tsp.	5 mL
Baking soda	1/2 tsp.	2 mL
Salt	1/2 tsp.	2 mL
Ground cinnamon	1/4 tsp.	1 mL
Butter (or hard margarine), softened	1/2 cup	125 mL
Granulated sugar	2/3 cup	150 mL
Large eggs	2	2
Sour cream	1/2 cup	125 mL
Vanilla extract	1 tsp.	5 mL
Coarsely chopped frozen whole raspberries	1 cup	250 mL

Measure first 5 ingredients into large bowl. Stir. Make a well in centre.

Cream butter and sugar in medium bowl. Add eggs, 1 at a time, beating well after each addition. Add sour cream and vanilla. Beat until smooth. Add to well in flour mixture.

Add raspberries. Stir until just moistened. Fill 12 greased muffin cups 3/4 full. Bake in 350°F (175°C) oven for 30 to 35 minutes until wooden pick inserted in centre of muffin comes out clean. Let stand in pan for 5 minutes. Remove muffins from pan and place on wire rack to cool. Makes 12 muffins.

1 muffin: 228 Calories; 10.1 g Total Fat (2.5 g Mono, 0.4 g Poly, 6.1 g Sat); 60 mg Cholesterol; 32 g Carbohydrate; 1 g Fibre; 4 g Protein; 241 mg Sodium

Pictured at right.

Get a leg up on the Christmas rush this year. The batter for these sweet gingerbread muffins can be made up to a month in advance and stored in an airtight container in your fridge. When guests are on their way, pop a batch in the oven and your house will be filled with the heavenly aromas of ginger, cloves and cinnamon.

tip

If there's no buttermilk on hand, make soured milk instead. Just measure 1 tbsp. (15 mL) of white vinegar or lemon juice into a 1 cup (250 mL) liquid measure. Add enough milk to make 1 cup (250 mL), then stir and let stand for 1 minute.

Batter-Ready Ginger Muffins

All-purpose flour	5 1/4 cups	1.3 L
Baking soda	1 tbsp.	15 mL
Ground cinnamon	1 1/2 tsp.	7 mL
Ground ginger	1 1/2 tsp.	7 mL
Salt	3/4 tsp.	4 mL
Ground nutmeg	1/2 tsp.	2 mL
Ground cloves	1/4 tsp.	1 mL
Butter (or hard margarine), softened	1 1/2 cups	375 mL
Granulated sugar	1 cup	250 mL
Large eggs	4	4
Fancy (mild) molasses	1 1/2 cups	375 mL
Buttermilk (or soured milk, see Tip)	1 cup	250 mL
Vanilla extract	1 1/2 tsp.	7 mL
Raisins	1 1/2 cups	375 mL

Measure first 7 ingredients into extra-large bowl. Stir. Make a well in centre.

Cream butter and sugar in large bowl. Add eggs, 1 at a time, beating well after each addition. Add next 3 ingredients. Beat until smooth. Add to well in flour mixture.

Add raisins. Stir until just moistened. Cover. Chill. Store in refrigerator for up to 1 month (see Note). When ready to bake, fill greased muffin cups 3/4 full. Bake in 375°F (190°C) oven for about 22 minutes until wooden pick inserted in centre of muffin comes out clean. Let stand in pan for 5 minutes. Remove muffins from pan and place on wire rack to cool. Makes about 36 muffins.

1 muffin: 215 Calories; 8.2 g Total Fat (2.0 g Mono, 0.3 g Poly, 5.0 g Sat); 44 mg Cholesterol; 34 g Carbohydrate; 1 g Fibre; 3 g Protein; 228 mg Sodium

Note: Once refrigerated, be careful not to over-stir the batter when spooning into muffin cups.

Breakfast Pull-Aparts

Granulated sugar	1/2 cup	125 mL
Ground cinnamon	1 tbsp.	15 mL
Frozen unbaked dinner rolls	20	20
Butter (or hard margarine), melted	1/4 cup	60 mL
Glazed red cherries, halved	1/2 cup	125 mL
Sliced almonds	1/2 cup	125 mL
Corn syrup	1/3 cup	75 mL
Butter (or hard margarine), melted	2 tbsp.	30 mL

These sweet and sticky cinnamon rolls are sure to be the star attraction of your Christmas breakfast! Put these together the night before so they're ready to go first thing in the morning.

Combine sugar and cinnamon in small bowl.

Dip rolls in first amount of butter. Roll in sugar mixture until coated. Arrange 10 rolls in greased 12 cup (3 L) bundt pan.

Sprinkle with half of cherries and half of almonds. Repeat with remaining rolls, cherries and almonds to make second layer.

Combine corn syrup and second amount of butter in small bowl. Drizzle over top. Cover with damp tea towel. Let stand at room temperature for at least 6 hours or overnight. Bake in 350°F (175°C) oven for about 30 minutes until golden. Loosen bread from pan and invert onto serving plate. Makes 20 pull-aparts.

1 pull-apart: 176 Calories; 6.7 g Total Fat (1.7 g Mono, 0.4 g Poly, 2.3 g Sat); 9 mg Cholesterol; 27 g Carbohydrate; 0 g Fibre; 4 g Protein; 173 mg Sodium

Pictured below.

christmas fun

What would Christmas Eve be without a viewing of Jimmy Stewart in *It's a Wonderful Life*? Surprisingly, this Frank Capra directed classic wasn't exactly well-received when it was first released in 1946. In fact, when its copyright expired almost 30 years later, no one was interested in renewing it! Because of this, television stations could air the movie for free. Stations took advantage of this fact and started annually airing the screen gem, and it found a whole new audience who loved the tale of hard-working, good-hearted George Bailey and his "beautiful old savings and loan."

Easy Cinnamon Knots

Water	2 2/3 cups	650 mL
Cooking oil	2/3 cup	150 mL
Granulated sugar	2/3 cup	150 mL
Salt	1 1/4 tsp.	6 mL
All-purpose flour	2 cups	500 mL
Instant yeast	2 tbsp.	30 mL
Large eggs, fork-beaten	4	4
All-purpose flour	7 cups	1.75 L
All-purpose flour, approximately	1/2 cup	125 mL
Granulated sugar	3 cups	750 mL
Ground cinnamon	3 tbsp.	50 mL
Butter (or hard margarine), melted	1 cup	250 mL

Combine first 4 ingredients in large saucepan. Heat and stir on medium until very warm and sugar is dissolved. Remove from heat.

Combine first amount of flour and yeast in extra-large bowl. Add warm water mixture. Mix until soft dough forms. Add eggs. Mix well.

Add second amount of flour, 1 cup (250 mL) at a time, mixing well after each addition until dough pulls away from sides of bowl. Turn out onto lightly floured surface. Knead for 5 to 10 minutes until smooth and elastic, adding third amount of flour 1 tbsp. (15 mL) at a time, if necessary, to prevent sticking. Place in greased extra-large bowl, turning once to grease top. Cover with greased waxed paper and tea towel. Let stand in oven with light on and door closed for about 25 minutes until doubled in bulk.

Combine second amount of sugar and cinnamon in medium bowl.

Punch dough down. Divide into 4 equal portions. Roll each portion into a rope. Cut each rope into 12 pieces. Roll each piece into a 10 inch (25 cm) long rope. Brush work surface with butter. Roll each rope in butter until coated, brushing work surface with more butter as necessary. Press ropes into sugar mixture until coated. Form into simple knots. Arrange 24 knots on greased baking sheet with sides. Arrange remaining knots on separate baking sheet. Cover with greased waxed paper and tea towel. Let stand in oven with light on and door closed for about 30 minutes until doubled in size. Bake on separate racks in 350°F (175°C) oven for 20 to 25 minutes, switching position of baking sheets at halftime, until golden. Makes 48 knots.

(continued on next page)

1 knot: 205 Calories; 7.2 g Total Fat (2.8 g Mono, 1.0 g Poly, 2.8 g Sat); 28 mg Cholesterol; 33 g Carbohydrate;
1 g Fibre; 3 g Protein; 94 mg Sodium

Pictured below.

Top: Easy Cinnamon Knots, page 10
Bottom: Biscuit Fruit Roll, page 12

For those who prefer just a small, sweet nibble at dawn's first light, this cream-filled quickbread is perfect to serve with Christmas morning's first coffee.

Biscuit Fruit Roll

PASTRY

All-purpose flour	2 cups	500 mL
Granulated sugar	1/3 cup	75 mL
Baking powder	4 tsp.	20 mL
Salt	1/2 tsp.	2 mL
Cold butter (or hard margarine), cut up	6 tbsp.	100 mL
Large egg	1	1
Milk	1/2 cup	125 mL

FILLING

Block of cream cheese, softened	4 oz.	125 g
Vanilla extract	1/2 tsp.	2 mL
Chopped mixed glazed fruit	1/2 cup	125 mL
Chopped walnuts	3 tbsp.	50 mL

COFFEE GLAZE

Cold strong prepared coffee	1 tbsp.	15 mL
Icing (confectioner's) sugar	1/2 cup	125 mL

Pastry: Combine first 4 ingredients in large bowl. Cut in butter until mixture resembles coarse crumbs. Make a well in centre.

Beat egg and milk with fork in small cup. Add to well. Stir until soft dough forms. Turn out onto lightly floured surface. Gently knead 4 or 5 times until dough just comes together. Roll or pat out to 8 x 8 inch (20 x 20 cm) square.

Filling: Mash cream cheese and vanilla with fork in small bowl until smooth. Spread on dough, leaving 1 inch (2.5 cm) border on top edge.

Sprinkle with glazed fruit and walnuts. Roll up from bottom, jelly roll-style. Pinch seam against roll to seal. Place, seam-side down, on greased baking sheet. Using sharp knife, cut 10 slashes across top of roll, about 1/2 inch (12 mm) deep. Bake in 425°F (220°C) oven for about 20 minutes until lightly browned. Remove roll from baking sheet and place on wire rack. Let stand for 10 minutes.

Coffee Glaze: Stir coffee into icing sugar in small bowl until smooth. Makes about 1/4 cup (60 mL) glaze. Drizzle over warm roll. Cuts into 10 slices.

1 slice: 295 Calories; 12.8 g Total Fat (3.1 g Mono, 1.5 g Poly, 7.2 g Sat); 53 mg Cholesterol; 41 g Carbohydrate; 1 g Fibre; 5 g Protein; 327 mg Sodium

Pictured on page 11.

Spiced Fruit Salad

Cubed honeydew	2 cups	500 mL
Halved seedless red grapes	2 cups	500 mL
Can of pineapple chunks, drained	14 oz.	398 mL
Can of sliced peaches in juice, drained and juice reserved, chopped	14 oz.	398 mL
Reserved peach juice		
Vanilla extract	1 tsp.	5 mL
Ground ginger	1/2 tsp.	2 mL
Ground allspice	1/4 tsp.	1 mL

Like many good things, this dish needs time. So, while visions of sugarplums dance in your loved ones' heads, let the sweet fruit steep in its spices and natural juices.

Combine first 4 ingredients in large bowl.

Combine remaining 4 ingredients in small bowl. Add to fruit mixture. Stir until coated. Chill, covered, for at least 6 hours or overnight. Makes about 6 cups (1.5 L).

1 cup (250 mL): 148 Calories; 0.3 g Total Fat (trace Mono, 0.1 g Poly, 0.1 g Sat); 0 mg Cholesterol; 39 g Carbohydrate; 3 g Fibre; 1 g Protein; 11.5 mg Sodium

Pictured on page 15.

Blueberries and vanilla make this French toast a delightfully sweet morning treat. Assemble these the night before because they have to chill in the fridge for at least six hours.

christmas fun

First released in 1966, the animated television special *Dr. Seuss' How the Grinch Stole Christmas* quickly became a beloved classic for young and old. Directed by Chuck Jones, one of the geniuses behind the Looney Tunes franchise, and narrated by Boris Karloff, best known for his B movie roles in horror films, it tells the tale of a green-skinned creature who can't enjoy Christmas because his heart is two sizes too small. In his attempt to steal Christmas from the Whos in the tiny town of Whoville, the Grinch learns the true meaning of Christmas, and his heart grows three sizes. The accompanying song *You're a Mean One, Mr. Grinch*, was sung, not by James Earl Jones, as many believe but by Thurl Ravenscroft, who was well-known for being the voice of Tony the Tiger in Kellogg's commercials.

Blueberry Streusel French Toast

Butter (or hard margarine)	1 tbsp.	15 mL
Texas bread slices	12	12
Large eggs	9	9
Milk	1 1/2 cups	375 mL
Granulated sugar	1 1/2 tbsp.	25 mL
Vanilla extract	1 tbsp.	15 mL
Salt	1/4 tsp.	1 mL
TOPPING		
Quick-cooking rolled oats	1 1/4 cups	300 mL
Brown sugar, packed	1/2 cup	125 mL
All-purpose flour	1/4 cup	60 mL
Grated lemon zest	1/2 tsp.	2 mL
Butter (or hard margarine)	1/3 cup	75 mL
Frozen (or fresh) blueberries	1 cup	250 mL

Grease 11 x 17 inch (28 x 43 cm) baking sheet with sides with first amount of butter.

Arrange bread slices in single layer on baking sheet.

Beat next 5 ingredients in large bowl until combined. Pour over bread slices.

Topping: Combine first 4 ingredients in medium bowl. Cut in butter until mixture resembles coarse crumbs. Sprinkle over bread slices.

Sprinkle blueberries over top. Chill, covered, for at least 6 hours or overnight. Bake, uncovered, in 450°F (230°C) oven for about 30 minutes until topping is crisp and golden around edges. Makes 12 French toast.

1 French toast: 322 Calories; 11.9 g Total Fat (1.7 g Mono, 0.2 g Poly, 6.1 g Sat); 179 mg Cholesterol; 43 g Carbohydrate; 2 g Fibre; 10 g Protein; 371 mg Sodium

Pictured at right.

Top: Spiced Fruit Salad, page 13
Bottom: Blueberry Streusel French Toast, above

Don't spend your Christmas morn cooking! Spend it doing better things— like opening presents. These easy eggs Benny can be made up to 12 hours in advance and then baked, so assemble them the night before so you can really focus on the next day's gift-giving!

christmas fun

Considered the most popular Christmas song of all time, *White Christmas* was written in 1940 by the famous song scribe Irving Berlin. It made its big silver screen debut in the movie Holiday Inn, starring crooner Bing Crosby and song and dance man Fred Astaire.

Make-Ahead Eggs Benedict

English muffins, split and toasted	4	4
Bacon slices, cooked crisp	16	16
Water, approximately	5 cups	1.25 L
White vinegar	1 tsp.	5 mL
Large eggs	8	8
SAUCE		
Butter (or hard margarine)	1/4 cup	60 mL
All-purpose flour	1/4 cup	60 mL
Paprika	1 tsp.	5 mL
Pepper	1/4 tsp.	1 mL
Ground nutmeg	1/8 tsp.	0.5 mL
Milk	2 cups	500 mL
Grated Swiss cheese	2 cups	500 mL
Dry (or alcohol-free) white wine	1/2 cup	125 mL
TOPPING		
Butter (or hard margarine)	1 tbsp.	15 mL
Cornflake crumbs	1/2 cup	125 mL

Arrange muffin halves, cut-side up, in greased 9 x 13 inch (22 x 33 cm) pan. Place 2 slices of bacon on each muffin half.

Pour water into large saucepan until about 1 1/2 inches (3.8 cm) deep. Add vinegar. Stir. Bring to a boil. Reduce heat to medium. Water should continue to simmer. Break 1 egg into shallow dish. Slip egg into water. Repeat with remaining eggs. Cook for 2 to 3 minutes until egg whites are set and slightly before yolks reach desired doneness (see Note 1). Remove eggs with slotted spoon. Place 1 egg on each muffin half.

Sauce: Melt butter in medium saucepan on medium. Add next 4 ingredients. Heat and stir for 1 minute.

Slowly add milk, stirring constantly with whisk, until boiling and thickened.

Add cheese and wine. Heat and stir until cheese is melted. Spoon sauce over eggs.

(continued on next page)

Topping: Melt butter in small saucepan on medium. Remove from heat. Add cornflake crumbs. Stir well. Sprinkle over sauce. Chill (see Note 2). Bake, uncovered, in 375°F (190°C) oven for 20 to 25 minutes until heated through. Serves 8.

1 serving: 574 Calories; 41.2 g Total Fat (11.4 g Mono, 2.7 g Poly, 18.2 g Sat); 293 mg Cholesterol; 25 g Carbohydrate; 1 g Fibre; 23 g Protein; 818 mg Sodium

Note 1: It is best to remove eggs from water slightly before desired doneness because the eggs will continue to cook as they bake.

Note 2: This recipe may be made ahead and chilled for up to 12 hours or baked immediately.

Best Hash Browns

Grated medium Cheddar cheese	2 cups	500 mL
Sour cream	2 cups	500 mL
Can of condensed cream of celery soup	10 oz.	284 mL
Can of condensed cream of chicken soup	10 oz.	284 mL
Butter (or hard margarine), melted	1/2 cup	125 mL
Onion flakes	3 tbsp.	50 mL
Seasoned salt	1 tsp.	5 mL
Frozen hash brown potatoes, partially thawed	2 lbs.	900 g
Cornflake crumbs	1/2 cup	125 mL

Combine first 7 ingredients in large bowl.

Add hash browns. Stir. Spread evenly in greased 9 x 13 inch (22 x 33 cm) baking dish.

Sprinkle cornflake crumbs over top. Bake, uncovered, in 350°F (175°C) oven for about 1 hour until heated through. Serves 12.

1 serving: 319 Calories; 23.2 g Total Fat (5.7 g Mono, 0.7 g Poly, 13.7 g Sat); 59 mg Cholesterol; 20 g Carbohydrate; 1 g Fibre; 9 g Protein; 658 mg Sodium

Pictured on page 19.

We don't throw around the word "best" lightly. These far-from-ordinary hash browns are made spectacular with the addition of a few simple ingredients.

christmas fun

Based on Mexican folklore, the legend of how the poinsettia became a Christmas flower is an endearing one. Clutching a paltry handful of weeds, a young peasant girl was making her way to church on Christmas day. The young girl wished she could give something more beautiful than her straggly gathering of weeds to show her love for the baby Jesus, but she knew her family could not afford any other offering. As a testament to her love and kind heart, the weeds miraculously transformed themselves into beautiful red flowers—poinsettias.

Delicious any time of year, but especially appealing for a Christmas morning brunch because it needs to be made ahead of time (all the better to relax and open gifts). Jalapeño cheese adds just enough heat to the sweet peppers and ham.

tip

You don't have to dry your bread cubes in the oven. If you have some time to spare, you can just leave the cubes out on the counter for a couple hours until they're sufficiently dry—it's an easy way to conserve energy.

Pepper And Ham Strata

Day-old unsliced white bread loaf, crust removed	1/2	1/2
Cooking oil	2 tsp.	10 mL
Finely chopped red onion	1/2 cup	125 mL
Chopped cooked ham	1 cup	250 mL
Chopped green pepper	1 cup	250 mL
Chopped red pepper	1 cup	250 mL
Grated jalapeño Monterey Jack cheese	2/3 cup	150 mL
Large eggs	8	8
Milk	2 cups	500 mL
Sour cream	1/3 cup	75 mL
Chopped fresh parsley (or 2 1/4 tsp., 11 mL, flakes)	3 tbsp.	50 mL
Honey Dijon mustard	2 tbsp.	30 mL
Salt	1/4 tsp.	1 mL
Pepper	1/4 tsp.	1 mL

Cut bread into 1/2 inch (12 mm) cubes. Spread in single layer on ungreased baking sheet with sides. Bake in 175°F (80°C) oven for about 30 minutes, turning occasionally, until dry. Spread cubes in greased 9 x 13 inch (22 x 33 cm) pan.

Heat cooking oil in small frying pan on medium. Add onion. Cook for about 5 minutes, stirring often, until softened. Scatter over bread cubes.

Sprinkle next 4 ingredients over onion.

Beat remaining 7 ingredients in large bowl until combined. Pour over cheese. Chill, covered, for at least 6 hours or overnight. Let stand at room temperature for 30 minutes. Bake, uncovered, in 350°F (175°C) oven for about 1 hour until golden, centre is raised and knife inserted in centre comes out clean. Puffiness will settle almost immediately. Serves 8.

1 serving: 392 Calories; 17.8 g Total Fat (2.2 g Mono, 0.6 g Poly, 5.4 g Sat); 248 mg Cholesterol; 40 g Carbohydrate; 1 g Fibre; 21 g Protein; 598 mg Sodium

Pictured at right.

Left: Pepper And Ham Strata, above
Right: Best Hash Browns, page 17

This festively coloured, alcohol-free punch is sure to be a favourite with kids of all ages.

tip

Just before serving, put a block of ice in your punch bowl to keep your punch nice and chilly throughout the party. You can freeze water in any empty plastic container or even a small jelly mold for a more decorative touch. Just make sure the block of ice will fit comfortably in your punch bowl.

Wassail (pronounced WAHS-uhl or WAHS-ayl) is a warming, spiced cider beverage that has been a traditional holiday favourite in England for centuries.

brandy wassail

If there's nary a kid in sight, you can spike your wassail by adding 1 cup (250 mL) of brandy or apple brandy near the end of the cooking time.

Christmas Punch

Cranberry cocktail	8 cups	2 L
Lemon lime soft drink	8 cups	2 L
Can of frozen concentrated lemonade, thawed	12 1/2 oz.	355 mL

Lime slices, for garnish
Maraschino cherries, for garnish
Orange slices, for garnish

Combine first 3 ingredients in punch bowl.

Garnish with lime slices, cherries, and orange slices. Makes about 18 cups (4.5 L).

1 cup (250 mL): 151 Calories; 0.1 g Total Fat (0 g Mono, trace Poly, trace Sat); 0 mg Cholesterol; 39 g Carbohydrate; trace Fibre; trace Protein; 16 mg Sodium

Pictured at right.

Slow Cooker Wassail

Apple cider	12 cups	3 L
Liquid honey (optional)	1/3 cup	75 mL
Cinnamon sticks (4 inches, 10 cm, each)	2	2
Whole allspice	12	12
Peel of small orange, white pith removed, chopped	1	1
Piece of gingerroot (1 inch, 2.5 cm length), chopped	1	1

Combine apple cider and honey in 4 quart (4 L) slow cooker.

Place cinnamon sticks and allspice in small resealable freezer bag. Pound with hammer or mallet until crushed. Transfer to 6 inch (15 cm) square of double-layered cheesecloth.

Add orange peel and ginger. Draw up corners and tie with butcher's string. Submerge in liquid in slow cooker. Cook, covered, on Low for about 6 hours or on High for about 3 hours until fragrant. Remove and discard spice bag. Makes about 12 1/2 cups (3.1 L).

1 cup (250 mL): 144 Calories; 0 g Total Fat (0 g Mono, 0 g Poly, 0 g Sat); 0 mg Cholesterol; 36 g Carbohydrate; 0 g Fibre; 0 g Protein; 24 mg Sodium

Pictured at right.

Instead of mulling over what to make for your cocktail party, make a batch of this full-bodied spiced wine. Double the batch if you're expecting a bigger crowd. Best served warm.

Mulled Wine

Cranberry cocktail	3 cups	750 mL
Liquid honey	1/4 cup	60 mL
Medium orange, sliced	1	1
Lemon slices	3	3
Cinnamon sticks (4 inches, 10 cm, each)	2	2
Whole cloves	10	10
Ground nutmeg	1/4 tsp.	1 mL
Dry (or alcohol-free) red wine	3 cups	750 mL

Combine first 7 ingredients in large saucepan. Cook, covered, on low for about 1 hour, stirring occasionally, until fragrant.

Add wine. Stir. Remove and discard orange slices, lemon slices, cinnamon sticks and cloves. Makes about 8 cups (2 L).

1/2 cup (125 mL): 81 Calories; trace Total Fat (0 g Mono, 0 g Poly, trace Sat); 0 mg Cholesterol; 12 g Carbohydrate; trace Fibre; trace Protein; 3 mg Sodium

Homemade Irish cream beats store-bought any day. You'll be amazed at how easy it is to create a fancy liqueur.

about raw eggs

Irish Cream uses raw eggs. Make sure to use fresh, clean Grade A eggs with no cracks. Keep chilled and consume the same day it is prepared. Always discard leftovers. Pregnant women, young children or the elderly are not advised to eat anything containing raw egg.

Irish Cream

Canadian whisky (rye)	1 1/2 cups	375 mL
Can of sweetened condensed milk	11 oz.	300 mL
Half-and-half cream	1 cup	250 mL
Large eggs	2	2
Chocolate milk powder	1 tsp.	5 mL
Instant coffee granules	1 tsp.	5 mL
Vanilla extract	1 tsp.	5 mL

Put all 7 ingredients into blender. Process until smooth. Pour into sterile glass jar with tight-fitting lid. Chill. Makes about 4 1/2 cups (1.1 L).

1 oz. (30 mL): 73 Calories; 2.1 g Total Fat (0.5 g Mono, 0.1 g Poly, 1.2 g Sat); 19 mg Cholesterol; 7 g Carbohydrate; 0 g Fibre; 1 g Protein; 22 mg Sodium

Pictured on page 21.

Christmas Spirit

Granulated sugar	2 cups	500 mL
Fresh (or frozen, thawed) raspberries	1 1/2 cups	375 mL
Fresh (or frozen, thawed) cranberries	1 1/3 cups	325 mL
Water	1 cup	250 mL
Orange juice	1/3 cup	75 mL
Cinnamon sticks (4 inches, 10 cm, each)	2	2
Grated orange zest (see Tip)	1 tbsp.	15 mL
Whole cloves	6	6
Whole allspice	4	4
Gin (or vodka)	3 cups	750 mL

Combine first 9 ingredients in Dutch oven or large pot. Bring to a boil on medium. Reduce heat to medium-low. Simmer, uncovered, for about 20 minutes until fragrant. Remove from heat. Cool to room temperature.

Add gin. Stir well. Pour into 2 sterile 4 cup (1 L) glass jars with tight-fitting lids. Let stand at room temperature for 2 weeks, shaking gently once every 2 days. Strain through sieve into 8 cup (2 L) liquid measure. Do not press. Gently lift berry mixture with spoon, allowing liquid to flow through sieve. Discard solids. Return liquid to same jars. Let stand at room temperature for 2 weeks. Strain liquid through double layer of cheesecloth into 2 cup (500 mL) liquid measure. Discard solids. Pour into sterile jar or decorative bottle with tight-fitting lid. Store at room temperature or in refrigerator for up to 1 month. Makes about 2 cups (500 mL).

1 oz. (30 mL): 192 Calories; trace Total Fat (0 g Mono, 0 g Poly, 0 g Sat); 0 mg Cholesterol; 25 g Carbohydrate; 0 g Fibre; trace Protein; 1 mg Sodium

Pictured on page 21.

Think Scrooge is the only one to be visited by Christmas spirits? This tart, yet sweet treat is guaranteed to drive the humbug away. Makes a great aperitif or after-dinner drink.

tip

When a recipe calls for grated lemon, orange or lime zest and juice, it's easier to grate first, and then juice. Be careful not to grate down to the pith (the white part of the peel), it's bitter and is best avoided.

It wouldn't be Christmas without eggnog. This homemade version comes with something store-bought nog doesn't have—a generous portion of spiced rum!

about raw eggs

Party Eggnog uses raw eggs. Make sure to use fresh, clean Grade A eggs with no cracks. Keep chilled and consume the same day it is prepared. Always discard leftovers. Pregnant women, young children or the elderly are not advised to eat anything containing raw egg.

Sugar and spice and everything nice!

tip

Always test your candy thermometer before each use. Simply bring some water to a boil and insert the thermometer. The water should reach a temperature of 212°F (100°C) at sea level. Adjust your recipe temperature up or down based on the test results. For example, if your thermometer reads 206°F (97°C), subtract 6°F (3°C) from each temperature called for in the recipe.

Party Eggnog

Large eggs	12	12
Icing (confectioner's) sugar	2 cups	500 mL
Vanilla extract	3 tbsp.	50 mL
Salt	1/2 tsp.	2 mL
Homogenized milk	8 cups	2 L
Spiced rum (or brandy)	1/2 – 1 cup	125 – 250 mL
Ground nutmeg	1 tsp.	5 mL
Ground cinnamon	1/2 tsp.	2 mL

Beat eggs in large bowl until frothy.

Add icing sugar, 1/4 cup (60 mL) at a time while beating, until combined. Add vanilla and salt. Stir. Pour into punch bowl.

Add remaining 4 ingredients. Stir well. Serve immediately. Makes about 14 cups (3.5 L).

1/2 cup (125 mL): 129 Calories; 4.3 g Total Fat (0.7 g Mono, 0.2 g Poly, 2.1 g Sat); 102 mg Cholesterol; 13 g Carbohydrate; trace Fibre; 5 g Protein; 106 mg Sodium

Pictured at right.

Candied Nuts

Granulated sugar	1 cup	250 mL
Milk	6 tbsp.	100 mL
Ground cinnamon	1 tsp.	5 mL
Unsalted mixed nuts (toasted, optional)	3 cups	750 mL
Vanilla extract	1/2 tsp.	2 mL

Combine first 3 ingredients in small heavy saucepan. Heat and stir on medium until boiling. Brush side of saucepan with wet pastry brush to dissolve any sugar crystals. Boil gently, without stirring, until mixture reaches firm ball stage (242° to 248°F, 117° to 120°C) on candy thermometer (see Tip) or until small amount dropped into very cold water forms a firm but pliable ball.

(continued on next page)

Add nuts and vanilla. Stir well. Transfer to greased baking sheet with sides. Separate nuts using fork. Let stand until cooled completely. Store in airtight container at room temperature for up to 1 week. Makes about 4 1/2 cups (1.1 L).

1/4 cup (60 mL): 180 Calories; 11.8 g Total Fat (7.2 g Mono, 2.5 g Poly, 1.6 g Sat); trace Cholesterol; 17 g Carbohydrate; 2 g Fibre; 4 g Protein; 6 mg Sodium

Pictured below.

Left: Party Eggnog, page 24
Right: Candied Nuts, page 24

This buttery-tasting, salty snack mix is great to have on hand for surprise visitors.

make ahead

Get a jump on Christmas by making Good Ol' Nuts 'N' Bolts ahead of time and storing it in the freezer for up to three months.

Good Ol' Nuts 'N' Bolts

Goldfish crackers	2 cups	500 mL
Rice squares cereal	2 cups	500 mL
Unsalted mixed nuts	2 cups	500 mL
Whole wheat squares cereal	2 cups	500 mL
"O"-shaped toasted oat cereal	1 cup	250 mL
Stick pretzels, broken in half	1 cup	250 mL
Butter (or hard margarine)	1/4 cup	60 mL
Cooking oil	1/4 cup	60 mL
Worcestershire sauce	2 tbsp.	30 mL
Celery salt	1 tsp.	5 mL
Garlic salt	1 tsp.	5 mL
Onion salt	1 tsp.	5 mL
Seasoned salt	1 tsp.	5 mL

Combine first 6 ingredients in large roasting pan.

Combine remaining 7 ingredients in small saucepan. Heat on medium, stirring occasionally, until butter is melted. Drizzle over cereal mixture. Toss until coated. Bake, uncovered, in 250°F (120°C) oven for 1 hour, stirring occasionally. Cool completely. Store in airtight containers at room temperature for up to 1 month. Makes about 8 cups (2 L).

1 cup (250 mL): 798 Calories; 43.1 g Total Fat (23.4 g Mono, 7.3 g Poly, 9.6 g Sat); 25 mg Cholesterol; 87 g Carbohydrate; 8 g Fibre; 17 g Protein; 1867 mg Sodium

Antipasto

Ketchup	1 1/4 cups	300 mL
Can of mushroom stems and pieces, drained and chopped	10 oz.	284 mL
Frozen cut green beans, chopped	1 cup	250 mL
Can of flaked light tuna in water, drained	6 oz.	170 g
Chopped dill pickle	1/2 cup	125 mL
Chopped green pepper	1/2 cup	125 mL
Chopped red pepper	1/2 cup	125 mL
Pickled onions, drained and halved	1/2 cup	125 mL
Pimiento-stuffed olives, chopped	1/2 cup	125 mL
Pitted whole black olives, chopped	1/2 cup	125 mL
Olive (or cooking) oil	2 tbsp.	30 mL
White vinegar	2 tbsp.	30 mL

Combine all 12 ingredients in large saucepan. Heat and stir on medium until boiling. Boil gently, uncovered, for 20 minutes, stirring often, to blend flavours. Cool completely. Store in airtight containers in freezer for up to 6 months. Makes about 6 1/2 cups (1.6 L).

2 tbsp. (30 mL): 29 Calories; 1.4 g Total Fat (0.6 g Mono, 0.3 g Poly, 0.1 g Sat); 1 mg Cholesterol; 3 g Carbohydrate; trace Fibre; 1 g Protein; 178 mg Sodium

Pictured below.

We've stuffed this tangy taste treat with olives galore! Serve with an assortment of crackers.

gift-giving tip

Feel free to make this party fave well before the Christmas season and freeze individual portions to give as host gifts. Make sure to label these gracious goodies with the instructions to keep refrigerated and use within a week of being thawed.

This rich cheese confection is sure to be the, dare we say it, belle of your ball. Make sure to have a decorative knife at the ready so guests can cut out slices. Serve with an assortment of crackers.

festive best cheeseball

Insert a little festive colouring into your cheese ball by adding 1 1/2 tsp. (7 mL) of chopped green pepper and 1 1/2 tsp. (7 mL) of chopped pimiento to the cream cheese mixture.

Cranberry and cheese are a delightful combination—the tartness of the cranberry adds a cheeky flair to the rich cheesy mixture. Serve with crackers and Melba toast.

Best Cheese Ball

Block of cream cheese, softened	8 oz.	250 g
Grated sharp Cheddar cheese	1 cup	250 mL
Worcestershire sauce	1 tsp.	5 mL
Onion flakes	1/2 tsp.	2 mL
Lemon juice	1/2 tsp.	2 mL
Salt, just a pinch		
Cayenne pepper, just a pinch		
Finely chopped pecans (or walnuts)	1/4 cup	60 mL

Beat first 7 ingredients in medium bowl until smooth. Shape into ball.

Spread pecans on plate. Roll and press ball in pecans until coated. Serves 12.

1 serving: 121 Calories; 11.5 g Total Fat (3.7 g Mono, 0.9 g Poly, 6.3 g Sat); 31 mg Cholesterol; 1 g Carbohydrate; trace Fibre; 4 g Protein; 119 mg Sodium

Cranberry Cheese

Grated sharp white Cheddar cheese, room temperature	2 cups	500 mL
Block of cream cheese, softened	4 oz.	125 g
Coarsely chopped dried cranberries	1/4 cup	60 mL

Beat Cheddar cheese and cream cheese in medium bowl until smooth.

Add cranberries. Mix well. Press into ungreased 1 1/2 cup (375 mL) mold or large cookie cutter, packing well to avoid air pockets. Chill, covered, for at least 3 hours until firm. Loosen cheese from mold and invert onto small serving plate. Serves 10.

1 serving: 137 Calories; 11.2 g Total Fat (1.1 g Mono, 0.1 g Poly, 6.5 g Sat); 36 mg Cholesterol; 4 g Carbohydrate; trace Fibre; 6 g Protein; 186 mg Sodium

Pictured at right.

Cranberry Cheese, above

The host that serves this rich spinach and artichoke dip will certainly be crowned the king (or queen) of the party. Great with French bread or tortilla chips.

King Artichoke Dip

Finely chopped onion	1 cup	250 mL
Bacon slices, diced	8	8
Garlic cloves, minced (or 1/2 tsp., 2 mL, powder)	2	2
Can of artichoke hearts, drained and chopped	14 oz.	398 mL
Block of cream cheese, softened	8 oz.	250 g
Sour cream	1/2 cup	125 mL
Finely chopped fresh spinach leaves, lightly packed	2 cups	500 mL
Worcestershire sauce	1/4 tsp.	1 mL

Heat large frying pan on medium. Add first 3 ingredients. Cook for about 5 minutes, stirring often, until bacon is browned and onion is softened.

Add artichoke. Heat and stir for 1 minute.

Beat cream cheese and sour cream in medium bowl until smooth. Add bacon mixture. Stir.

Add spinach and Worcestershire sauce. Stir well. Makes about 3 cups (750 mL).

2 tbsp. (30 mL): 54 Calories; 4.7 g Total Fat (2.3 g Mono, 0.5 g Poly, 2.9 g Sat); 11 mg Cholesterol; 2 g Carbohydrate; trace Fibre; 1 g Protein; 76 mg Sodium

Add a little bit of South Asia to your party fare with this not-too-spicy dip packed with crab and shrimp. Serve with crackers or cut-up fresh veggies.

make ahead

Save yourself some stress by making this dip up to 24 hours in advance and storing it in an airtight container in the fridge.

Seafood Curry Dip

Cream cheese, softened	1/4 cup	60 mL
Mayonnaise	1/4 cup	60 mL
Finely chopped green onion	2 tbsp.	30 mL
Curry powder	2 tsp.	10 mL
Lime juice	1 1/2 tsp.	7 mL
Can of crabmeat, drained, cartilage removed, flaked	4 1/4 oz.	120 g
Coarsely chopped cooked salad shrimp	3/4 cup	175 mL

(continued on next page)

Mash cream cheese with fork in large bowl. Add next 4 ingredients. Mix well.

Add crab and shrimp. Stir well. Chill until ready to serve. Makes about
1 1/3 cups (325 mL).

1 tbsp. (15 mL): 37 Calories; 2.9 g Total Fat (1.2 g Mono, 0.8 g Poly, 0.8 g Sat); 11 mg Cholesterol;
1 g Carbohydrate; trace Fibre; 2 g Protein; 78 mg Sodium

Pictured below.   Seafood Curry Dip, page 30

This sophisticated appetizer has a subtle blue cheese and bacon flavour.

make ahead

Make these pretty puffs a month in advance and freeze them in an airtight container until the day of your party. To reheat, pop the frozen puffs into a 350°F (175°C) oven for about 5 minutes until hot.

Stilton Puffs

Water	1 cup	250 mL
Butter (or hard margarine)	1/2 cup	125 mL
Salt	1/8 tsp.	0.5 mL
All-purpose flour	1 cup	250 mL
Large eggs	4	4
Crumbled Stilton cheese	4 oz.	113 g
Bacon slices, cooked crisp and crumbled	8	8
Finely chopped green onion	1/4 cup	60 mL
Pepper	1/2 tsp.	2 mL

Combine first 3 ingredients in medium heavy saucepan on medium-high until boiling and butter is melted. Reduce heat to medium.

Add flour. Stir vigorously for about 1 minute until mixture pulls away from side of saucepan to form soft dough. Remove from heat. Transfer to medium bowl.

Add eggs, 1 at a time, beating after each addition until well combined and dough is thick and glossy.

Add remaining 4 ingredients. Mix. Drop, using 2 tsp. (10 mL) for each, about 2 inches (5 cm) apart onto greased baking sheet with sides. Bake in 425°F (220°C) oven for 15 to 17 minutes until golden brown. Let stand on baking sheet for 5 minutes. Remove puffs from baking sheet and place on wire racks to cool. Makes about 72 puffs.

1 puff: 30 Calories; 2.2 g Total Fat (0.5 g Mono, 0.1 g Poly, 1.3 g Sat); 17 mg Cholesterol; 1 g Carbohydrate; trace Fibre; 1 g Protein; 52 mg Sodium

Pictured at right.

Top: Crisp Almond Pepper Bread, page 34
Bottom: Stilton Puffs, above

Kick up your cheese platter with this crisp, peppery bread (think of a savoury biscotti). The flavour combination is fantastic!

make ahead

This recipe can be made in advance and stored in an airtight container at room temperature for up to one week or in the freezer for up to one month.

Crisp Almond Pepper Bread

Egg whites (large)	2	2
Granulated sugar	1/3 cup	75 mL
All-purpose flour	3/4 cup	175 mL
Ground allspice	1/2 tsp.	2 mL
Whole natural almonds	1 cup	250 mL
Coarsely ground pepper	1 1/2 tsp.	7 mL

Beat egg whites and sugar in medium bowl for about 5 minutes until soft peaks form.

Combine flour and allspice in small bowl. Add to egg white mixture. Stir.

Fold in almonds and pepper until evenly distributed. Line bottom and sides of greased 8 x 4 x 3 inch (20 x 10 x 7.5 cm) loaf pan with parchment (not waxed) paper. Spread batter in pan. Bake in 350°F (175°C) oven for about 35 minutes until golden. Let stand in pan on wire rack for 1 hour. Remove loaf from pan and place on wire rack to cool completely. Using serrated knife, cut loaf into 1/4 inch (6 mm) slices. Arrange slices about 1 inch (2.5 cm) apart on ungreased baking sheet with sides. Bake in 300°F (150°C) oven for about 20 minutes, turning at halftime, until dry and crisp. Makes about 32 slices.

1 slice: 45 Calories; 2.2 g Total Fat (1.4 g Mono, 0.5 g Poly, 0.2 g Sat); 0 mg Cholesterol; 5 g Carbohydrate; 1 g Fibre; 1 g Protein; 3 mg Sodium

Pictured on page 33.

Get caught up in the holiday whirl with these cranberry and feta-filled tortilla rolls.

green onion whirls

Add the same amount of green onion instead of mint to put a whole new spin on these whirls.

Holiday Whirls

Crumbled feta cheese (about 8 oz., 225 g), room temperature	1 3/4 cups	425 mL
Block of cream cheese, softened	8 oz.	250 g
Chopped dried cranberries	1 cup	250 mL
Finely chopped fresh mint	1/4 cup	60 mL
Spinach flour tortillas (9 inch, 22 cm diameter)	5	5

(continued on next page)

Beat feta and cream cheese in medium bowl until smooth. Add cranberries and mint. Stir well.

Spread cheese mixture evenly on tortillas, almost to edge. Roll up tightly, jelly roll-style. Wrap rolls with plastic wrap. Chill for at least 6 hours or overnight. Trim ends. Cut each roll diagonally into 8 slices. Makes 40 slices.

1 slice: 69 Calories; 3.5 g Total Fat (0.9 g Mono, 0.2 g Poly, 1.9 g Sat); 9 mg Cholesterol; 7 g Carbohydrate; 1 g Fibre; 2 g Protein; 121 mg Sodium

Simple Stuffed Mushrooms

Medium fresh white mushrooms	16	16
Butter (or hard margarine)	1/4 cup	60 mL
Finely chopped onion	1/4 cup	60 mL
Salt	1/4 tsp.	1 mL
Pepper	1/8 tsp.	0.5 mL
Fine dry bread crumbs	1/2 cup	125 mL

Remove stems from mushrooms. Chop stems. Arrange caps, stem-side up, on baking sheet with sides.

Combine next 4 ingredients and stems in medium frying pan. Cook on medium for about 5 minutes, stirring often, until onion is clear and soft.

Add bread crumbs. Stir. Spoon crumb mixture into caps. Bake in 350°F (175°C) oven for 10 to 15 minutes until mushrooms are tender. Serve immediately. Makes 16 stuffed mushrooms.

1 stuffed mushroom: 43 Calories; 3.1 g Total Fat (0.8 g Mono, 0.2 g Poly, 1.8 g Sat); 8 mg Cholesterol; 3 g Carbohydrate; trace Fibre; 1 g Protein; 87 mg Sodium

Reduce the stress of your holiday cocktail party preparations by making this super-simple but very elegant appetizer.

time-saving tip

Instead of baking, these tasty mushrooms can be broiled for about five minutes.

blue stuffed mushrooms

Give these tasty appetizers a strong cheese flavour by adding 1/4 cup (60 mL) crumbled blue cheese in with the bread crumbs.

These elegantly decadent tarts are an absolutely wonderful addition to your cocktail party menu! Use a crinkle-edged cookie cutter to cut out your pastry for an even prettier presentation.

time-saving tip

Cut out a step and use prepared mini-tart shells instead of making your own pastry.

Crab Tarts

CREAM CHEESE PASTRY

Butter (or hard margarine), softened	1/4 cup	60 mL
Block of cream cheese, softened	4 oz.	125 g
All-purpose flour	3/4 cups	175 mL
Dried dillweed	1/2 tsp.	2 mL

FILLING

Large eggs	3	3
Grated Havarti (or Swiss) cheese	1 cup	250 mL
Can of crabmeat, drained, cartilage removed, flaked	4 1/4 oz.	120 g
Minced onion flakes	1 tsp.	5 mL
Parsley flakes	1 tsp.	5 mL
Worcestershire sauce	1/4 tsp.	1 mL
Salt	1/4 tsp.	1 mL
Pepper	1/8 tsp.	0.5 mL

Paprika (optional), sprinkle

Cream Cheese Pastry: Beat butter and cream cheese in large bowl until smooth. Add flour and dill. Mix well. Form into a ball. Chill for 1 hour.

Filling: Beat eggs in large bowl until frothy. Add next 7 ingredients. Mix well. Roll out pastry on lightly floured surface to about 1/8 inch (3 mm) thickness. Cut out circles with lightly floured 2 1/2 inch (6.4 cm) round cookie cutter. Press circles into bottom and sides of ungreased mini-muffin cups. Spoon filling into cups.

Sprinkle with paprika. Bake in 400°F (205°C) oven for about 15 minutes until golden and set. Makes about 24 tarts.

1 tart: 77 Calories; 5.5 g Total Fat (1.0 g Mono, 0.1 g Poly, 3.3 g Sat); 41 mg Cholesterol; 3 g Carbohydrate; trace Fibre; 3 g Protein; 106 mg Sodium

Pictured at right.

Glazed Meatballs

Chopped onion (or 2 tsp., 10 mL, flakes)	1/4 cup	60 mL
Fine dry bread crumbs	1/4 cup	60 mL
Water	1/4 cup	60 mL
Ground cinnamon	1/2 tsp.	2 mL
Salt	1 tsp.	5 mL
Pepper	1/4 tsp.	1 mL
Lean ground beef	1 1/2 lbs.	680 g
Grape jelly	1 1/2 cups	375 mL
Ketchup	1/2 cup	125 mL

Combine first 6 ingredients in large bowl.

Add beef. Mix well. Roll into 1 inch (2.5 cm) balls.

Combine jelly and ketchup in large frying pan. Heat and stir on medium until jelly is melted. Add meatballs. Cook, uncovered, for 20 to 25 minutes, stirring at halftime, until meatballs are fully cooked and internal temperature reaches 160°F (71°C). Makes about 48 meatballs.

1 meatball with 1 1/2 tsp. (7 mL) sauce: 55 Calories; 1.5 g Total Fat (0.6 g Mono, 0.1 g Poly, 0.6 g Sat); 9 mg Cholesterol; 8 g Carbohydrate; trace Fibre; 3 g Protein; 93 mg Sodium

Coated in a sweet and tangy glaze, these tender meatballs are very popular party fare.

crabapple meatballs

For a more subtle glaze, use crabapple jelly instead of grape.

Crab Tarts, page 36

It's not called Shrimp Cocktail because it's great served at tea parties! This delightful standard is a must have at any cocktail-enhanced shindig.

Shrimp Cocktail

Butter lettuce leaves		
Frozen, cooked large shrimp (peeled and deveined), thawed, tails intact	48	48
SEAFOOD SAUCE		
Chili sauce	1/2 cup	125 mL
Ketchup	1/3 cup	75 mL
Sweet pickle relish	2 tbsp.	30 mL
Prepared horseradish	1 tsp.	5 mL
Lemon juice	1/2 tsp.	2 mL
Worcestershire sauce	1/2 tsp.	2 mL
Seasoned salt	1/4 tsp.	1 mL

Line 8 shallow cocktail glasses or small glass bowls with lettuce leaves. Place 6 shrimp around top outside edge of each glass with tails hanging down.

Seafood Sauce: Combine all 7 ingredients in small bowl. Makes about 3/4 cup (175 mL) sauce. Spoon about 1 1/2 tbsp. (25 mL) sauce into centre of each glass. Makes 8 shrimp cocktails.

1 shrimp cocktail: 116 Calories; 0.6 g Total Fat (0.2 g Mono, 0.2 g Poly, 0.1 g Sat); 64 mg Cholesterol; 22 g Carbohydrate; 1 g Fibre; 7 g Protein; 1037 mg Sodium

Pictured below.

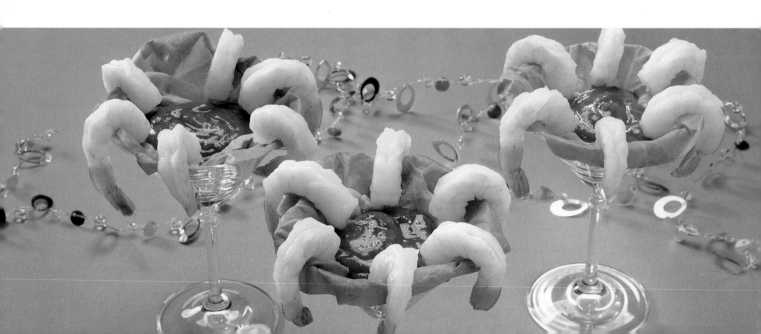

Lobster Chowder

Butter (or hard margarine)	1/4 cup	60 mL
Chopped onion	1 1/2 cups	375 mL
Diced celery	1 cup	250 mL
Diced green pepper	3/4 cup	175 mL
All-purpose flour	1/4 cup	60 mL
Diced peeled potato	2 1/2 cups	625 mL
Water	2 1/2 cups	625 mL
Salt	1 3/4 tsp.	9 mL
Pepper	1/4 tsp.	1 mL
Haddock fillets, any small bones removed, cut into bite-sized pieces	1 lb.	454 g
Can of frozen lobster meat, thawed (with liquid)	11.3 oz.	320 g
Fresh (or frozen, thawed) small bay scallops	1/2 lb.	225 g
Can of evaporated milk	13 1/2 oz.	385 mL
Homogenized milk	1 1/2 cups	375 mL

Melt butter in medium frying pan on medium. Add next 3 ingredients. Cook for about 10 minutes, stirring often, until vegetables are softened.

Sprinkle with flour. Heat and stir for 1 minute.

Combine next 4 ingredients in Dutch oven or large pot. Stir. Bring to a boil. Reduce heat to medium. Boil gently, covered, for about 10 minutes until potatoes are tender-crisp. Add flour mixture. Heat and stir until boiling and starting to thicken.

Add next 3 ingredients. Stir. Cook for 5 to 10 minutes until fish flakes easily when tested with fork.

Add evaporated milk and milk. Heat and stir until hot, but not boiling. Makes about 11 1/2 cups (2.9 L).

1 cup (250 mL): 218 Calories; 6.4 g Total Fat (1.7 g Mono, 0.5 g Poly, 3.7 g Sat); 67 mg Cholesterol; 18 g Carbohydrate; 1 g Fibre; 22 g Protein; 617 mg Sodium

This elegant chowder, packed with seafood, is the perfect choice for a very special Christmas Eve supper. This recipe makes an extra-big batch but be warned—everyone will want seconds! If you can't find frozen canned lobster in your grocery store, you'll find it in a fish market.

christmas fun

While doing your Christmas shopping, you may have noticed some rather peculiar pickle ornaments—in fact, you may even own one. Where the custom of the Christmas pickle came from is up for debate. Some people believe it is a German tradition—much to the surprise of many Germans! Others believe the custom originated in the United States during their civil war. Some even think it is a modern hoax. Either way, the purpose of the pickle is clear. The pickle owner is supposed to hide it well on the Christmas tree, and the first person to spot it is said to be granted good luck for an entire year.

These decadent, plated scallop salads are perfect for a very special holiday evening.

about scallops

Scallops are molluscs with wavy, fan-shaped shells—which is where the term "scalloped edge" comes from. They should range in colour from beige to creamy pink and should have a seawater smell to them. If scallops are white and odourless, they have most likely been soaked in a solution that plumps them up and increases their longevity. If your scallops appear sandy, give them a brief rinse but do not soak them because they'll absorb too much water. Scallops are notoriously easy to overcook and should never be cooked longer than indicated in a recipe.

Scallop Attraction

Butter (or hard margarine)	2 tbsp.	30 mL
Small zucchini (with peel), thinly sliced	2	2
Medium tomatoes, halved, seeded and diced	3	3
Dried oregano	1/4 tsp.	1 mL
Dried basil	1/8 tsp.	0.5 mL
Dry (or alcohol-free) white wine	1/4 cup	60 mL
Fresh (or frozen, thawed) large sea scallops, cut into 3 slices each	1 lb.	454 g
Butter (or hard margarine)	2 tbsp.	30 mL
All-purpose flour	2 tbsp.	30 mL
Half-and-half cream (or evaporated milk)	2/3 cup	150 mL
Diced red pepper (or pimiento), for garnish		

Melt first amount of butter in medium frying pan on medium. Add zucchini. Cook for about 5 minutes, stirring occasionally, until lightly browned. Transfer to plate. Cover to keep warm.

Add tomatoes to same frying pan. Heat and stir for 1 to 2 minutes until tomato skin starts to wrinkle. Sprinkle with oregano and basil. Stir. Transfer to separate plate. Cover to keep warm.

Add wine to same frying pan. Bring to a boil on medium. Add scallops. Cook for 1 to 2 minutes, stirring occasionally, until scallops are opaque. Transfer scallops to separate plate using slotted spoon. Cover to keep warm. Pour pan liquid into 1 cup (250 mL) liquid measure.

Melt second amount of butter in small saucepan on medium. Add flour. Heat and stir for 1 minute.

Slowly add reserved pan liquid, stirring constantly with whisk. Slowly add cream, stirring constantly with whisk, until boiling and thickened. Arrange zucchini slices, slightly overlapping, in a circle on 4 individual salad plates. Spoon tomato mixture onto centre of zucchini slices. Arrange scallop slices in a circle over tomatoes. Place 1 scallop slice in centre of each circle. Pour 1/4 cup (60 mL) cream mixture over each salad.

Garnish with red pepper. Serves 4.

1 serving: 315 Calories; 17.5 g Total Fat (4.4 g Mono, 1.0 g Poly, 10.3 g Sat); 83 mg Cholesterol; 15 g Carbohydrate; 2 g Fibre; 22 g Protein; 290 mg Sodium

Pictured at right.

Don't let your leftover turkey bones go to waste—they make for an excellent soup! Add some extra cut-up turkey meat at the end if you have any left over.

Turkey Mixed Bean Soup

Leftover turkey carcass	1	1
Water	12 cups	3 L
Bay leaves	2	2
Large onion, chopped	1	1
Celery ribs (with leaves), chopped	2	2
Medium carrots, chopped	3	3
Can of mixed beans (with liquid)	19 oz.	540 mL
Can of diced tomatoes (with juice)	14 oz.	398 mL
Chicken bouillon powder	1 tbsp.	15 mL
Dried oregano	1 tsp.	5 mL
Salt	1 tsp.	5 mL
Pepper	1/4 tsp.	1 mL

Break up turkey carcass to fit in Dutch oven or large pot. Add water and bay leaves. Bring to a boil. Reduce heat to medium-low. Simmer, covered, for 1 1/2 hours. Skim and discard foam from side of pot. Remove turkey carcass. Remove turkey from bones. Discard bones. Chop turkey. Strain stock through sieve into extra-large bowl. Discard solids.

Combine remaining 9 ingredients, stock and turkey in same Dutch oven. Bring to a boil. Reduce heat to medium-low. Simmer, uncovered, for 30 to 45 minutes, stirring occasionally, until vegetables are tender. Makes about 19 cups (4.75 L).

1 cup (250 mL): 47 Calories; 0.5 g Total Fat (0.2 g Mono, 0.2 g Poly, 0.1 g Sat); 3 mg Cholesterol; 7 g Carbohydrate; 2 g Fibre; 3 g Protein; 482 mg Sodium

Pictured at right.

Start your dinner party off right with this delicate lettuce and luscious fruit salad, topped with a creamy dressing.

make ahead

Prepare this sweet and tangy dressing up to two days in advance and store in an airtight container in the fridge.

Mandarin Poppy Seed Salad

Cut or torn butter lettuce (or mixed salad greens), lightly packed	8 cups	2 L
Can of mandarin orange segments, drained and syrup reserved	10 oz.	284 mL
Seedless red grapes, halved	1 cup	250 mL
Thinly sliced red onion	1/4 cup	60 mL
ORANGE POPPY SEED DRESSING		
Liquid honey	3 tbsp.	50 mL
Apple cider vinegar	2 tbsp.	30 mL
Cooking oil	2 tbsp.	30 mL
Reserved mandarin orange syrup	2 tbsp.	30 mL
Dijon mustard	1 tbsp.	15 mL
Poppy seeds	1 tsp.	5 mL
Pepper, sprinkle		

Put first 4 ingredients into large bowl.

Orange Poppy Seed Dressing: Put all 7 ingredients into blender. Process until smooth. Makes about 1/2 cup (125 mL) dressing. Drizzle over salad. Toss gently. Makes about 8 cups (2 L).

1 cup (250 mL): 104 Calories; 3.8 g Total Fat (2.0 g Mono, 1.1 g Poly, 0.3 g Sat); 0 mg Cholesterol; 17 g Carbohydrate; 1 g Fibre; 1 g Protein; 31 mg Sodium

Pictured at right.

A jellied salad is a must-have holiday dish. This refreshing and creamy treat is perfect for a special luncheon.

about jelly molds

The fun thing about jellied salads is that they can be molded into almost any shape you can imagine. Stores sell molds in the shapes of animals, Christmas trees and snowmen, to name just a few. So have some fun with your jellied salad and get yourself a mold that reflects the occasion and your personality.

Lime Pear Salad

Boxes of lime jelly powder (gelatin), 3 oz. (85 g) each	2	2
Boiling water	1 cup	250 mL
Block of cream cheese, cut up and softened	4 oz.	125 g
Reserved pear juice	1 cup	250 mL
Can of pear halves in juice, drained and juice reserved, diced	28 oz.	796 mL
Miniature multi-colored marshmallows (or 10 large marshmallows, cut up)	1 1/4 cups	300 mL
Whipping cream	1 cup	250 mL

Stir jelly powder into boiling water in large heatproof bowl until dissolved.

Add cream cheese, a few pieces at a time, stirring constantly, until melted. Add reserved pear juice. Stir. Chill for about 1 hour, stirring occasionally, until mixture starts to thicken.

Fold in pear and marshmallows.

Beat whipping cream in small bowl on medium-high until soft peaks form. Fold into gelatin mixture. Pour into 6 cup (1.5 L) mold or serving bowl. Chill for about 90 minutes until firm. Serves 12.

1 serving: 219 Calories; 10.3 g Total Fat (3.0 g Mono, 0.4 g Poly, 6.4 g Sat); 36 mg Cholesterol; 31 g Carbohydrate; 1 g Fibre; 3 g Protein; 110 mg Sodium

Pictured below.

Turkey À La King

Butter (or hard margarine)	2 tbsp.	30 mL
Sliced fresh white mushrooms	1 cup	250 mL
Diced red pepper	1/4 cup	60 mL
Butter (or hard margarine)	2 tbsp.	30 mL
All-purpose flour	1/4 cup	60 mL
Salt	1/2 tsp.	2 mL
Pepper	1/4 tsp.	1 mL
Cayenne pepper	1/8 tsp.	0.5 mL
Dry sherry	1 tbsp.	15 mL
Milk	2 cups	500 mL
Diced cooked turkey	2 cups	500 mL
Frozen peas	3/4 cup	175 mL

Melt first amount of butter in large frying pan on medium-high. Add mushrooms and red pepper. Cook for about 3 minutes, stirring often, until mushrooms are soft.

Add second amount of butter. Heat and stir until melted. Add next 4 ingredients. Heat and stir for 1 minute.

Add sherry. Slowly add milk, stirring constantly with whisk, until boiling and thickened.

Add turkey and peas. Stir. Reduce heat to low. Cook and stir until heated through. Makes about 4 cups (1 L).

1 cup (250 mL): 382 Calories; 15.8 g Total Fat (4.1 g Mono, 1.4 g Poly, 9.0 g Sat); 150 mg Cholesterol; 17 g Carbohydrate; 2 g Fibre; 41 g Protein; 546 mg Sodium

Pictured above.

Christmas dinner is finished and you're left with a fridge full of turkey. Consider yourself lucky. With this simple recipe, Boxing Day dinner is sure to be a hit!

serving suggestion

Make your Turkey À La King fit for a king (or queen) by serving it in puff pastry patty shells, which can be found at your local grocer's.

Pictured above.

If your family is getting a little tired of leftovers, make up some of these pot pies and freeze them for another day. You can use up your leftover gravy, turkey and mixed vegetables all in one go.

christmas fun

In Dickens' *A Christmas Carol*, it is a Christmas goose that the reformed Scrooge sends to his mistreated employee Bob Cratchit, not a turkey. Goose is still a popular Christmas entree in some European countries, but turkey's popularity is international. Perhaps one of the best traditions associated with Christmas turkey is the battle of the wishbone. Once the wishbone is dried, two people pull on the ends until it snaps, and the one who ends up with the biggest piece is guaranteed good luck.

Turkey Pies

FILLING

Turkey gravy	1 3/4 cups	425 mL
Minced onion flakes	2 tsp.	10 mL
Salt	1/4 tsp.	1 mL
Pepper	1/8 tsp.	0.5 mL
Poultry seasoning	1/8 tsp.	0.5 mL
Prepared chicken broth	1/4 cup	60 mL
Diced cooked turkey	2 2/3 cups	650 mL
Cooked mixed vegetables, chopped	1 cup	250 mL
Jar of pimiento, well drained and chopped	2 oz.	57 mL

PIES

Pastry for 2 double crust 9 inch (22 cm) pies		
Large egg, fork-beaten	1	1

Filling: Combine first 5 ingredients in medium bowl. Add broth, 1 tbsp. (15 mL) at a time, stirring constantly, until medium-thin consistency.

Add next 3 ingredients. Stir well.

Pies: Divide 2/3 of pastry into 6 equal portions. Roll out portions, 1 at a time, on lightly floured surface to about 1/8 inch (3 mm) thickness. Line six 4 3/8 inch (11 cm) foil pot pie pans. Spoon filling into shells. Divide remaining pastry into 6 equal portions. Roll out portions, 1 at a time, on lightly floured surface to about 1/8 inch (3 mm) thickness. Brush edges of shells with egg. Cover filling with pastry. Trim and crimp edges to seal. Brush tops of pies with remaining egg. Cut 3 or 4 small slits in tops to allow steam to escape. Place pies on baking sheet. Bake on bottom rack in 400°F (205°C) oven for about 30 minutes until browned. Makes 6 pies.

1 pie: 543 Calories; 23.0 g Total Fat (0.6 g Mono, 0.9 g Poly, 9.2 g Sat); 149 mg Cholesterol; 46 g Carbohydrate; 2 g Fibre; 36 g Protein; 956 mg Sodium

Pictured at right.

Add some flair to your glazed ham by using redcurrant jelly—it makes for a pleasant twist on the traditional. The leftovers make exceptional sandwiches.

Redcurrant And Mustard-Glazed Ham

GLAZE

Redcurrant jelly	1/2 cup	125 mL
Apple cider vinegar	1/4 cup	60 mL
Dry mustard	1 tbsp.	15 mL

HAM

Cooked bone-in ham	9 lbs.	4 kg
Whole cloves, approximately	3 tbsp.	50 mL

Glaze: Combine all 3 ingredients in small saucepan. Heat and stir on medium for about 5 minutes until jelly is dissolved.

Ham: Score ham in diamond shape pattern, about 1/4 inch (6 mm) deep with sharp knife. Stick whole clove into centre of each diamond shape in ham. Place ham on wire rack set in large roasting pan. Bake, uncovered, in 325°F (160°C) oven for 1 hour. Brush with glaze. Bake for another 30 to 45 minutes, brushing several times with glaze, until ham is glazed and internal temperature reaches 140°F (60°C). Serves 16.

1 serving: 382 Calories; 24.5 g Total Fat (11.5 g Mono, 2.6 g Poly, 8.7 g Sat); 90 mg Cholesterol; 7 g Carbohydrate; 0 g Fibre; 31 g Protein; 1749 mg Sodium

Pictured at right.

This sweet sauce with plump raisins is a special treat with baked ham or pork roast.

Raisin Sauce

Hot water	2 cups	500 mL
Raisins	1/2 cup	125 mL
Brown sugar, packed	1 1/3 cups	325 mL
Water	1/2 cup	125 mL
Cornstarch	1/4 cup	60 mL
White vinegar	3 tbsp.	50 mL
Dry mustard	1/4 tsp.	1 mL

Combine hot water and raisins in medium saucepan. Let stand for 1 hour.

Add remaining 5 ingredients. Heat and stir on medium until boiling and thickened. Makes about 3 1/4 cups (800 mL).

1/4 cup (60 mL): 114 Calories; trace Total Fat (0 g Mono, trace Poly, trace Sat); 0 mg Cholesterol; 29 g Carbohydrate; trace Fibre; trace Protein; 12 mg Sodium

Redcurrant And Mustard-Glazed Ham, page 50

What would the holidays be without turkey? And nothing's easier! With this simple recipe, you're guaranteed success.

about cooking turkey

The following tips will help make your turkey dinner a safe success:

- Thaw the turkey, breast-side up, on a tray in the refrigerator. Allow five hours per pound or ten hours per kilogram.

- Once thawed, remove the giblets and neck from the cavity. Discard, cook or store in an airtight container in the fridge.

- Wash hands, utensils, cutting boards, countertops and sink with hot, soapy water after handling raw turkey. Use paper towels for cleanup.

- Discard all wrapping used to store the raw turkey.

Roast Turkey

Medium onion, quartered (see Note)	1	1
Whole turkey, giblets and neck removed (not self-basting)	12 – 15 lbs.	5.4 – 6.8 kg
Cooking oil	2 tbsp.	30 mL

Place onion in body cavity of turkey. Tie wings with butcher's string close to body. Tie legs to tail. Place on greased wire rack set in large roasting pan.

Rub cooking oil over surface of turkey. Bake, covered, in 325°F (160°C) oven for 3 1/4 hours. Bake, uncovered, for about 15 minutes until browned and meat thermometer inserted into thickest part of thigh reads 165°F (74°C). Remove turkey from oven. Cover with foil. Let stand for 15 minutes before carving. Serves 12 to 16.

1 serving: 597 Calories; 31.0 g Total Fat (11.7 g Mono, 7.8 g Poly, 8.3 g Sat); 244 mg Cholesterol; 1 g Carbohydrate; trace Fibre; 73 g Protein; 233 mg Sodium

Pictured on front cover and at right.

Note: If you're going to stuff your turkey, omit onion.

Turkey roasting times

There are general guidelines for how long turkeys of certain weights should be cooked, but it is important to know that **a turkey is only truly cooked when it reaches its safe internal temperature**. Cooking times can vary based on how many times the oven door is opened, the size of the oven in relation to the turkey, whether the oven is a convection oven or a standard oven...the list goes on and on! So, although the following chart can be used as a guideline, it won't tell you when your turkey is done—you must use a meat thermometer for that.

size	without stuffing	with stuffing
6 – 8 lbs (3 – 3.5 kg)	2 1/2 – 2 3/4 hours	3 – 3 1/4 hours
8 – 10 lbs (3.5 – 4.5 kg)	2 3/4 – 3 hours	3 1/4 – 3 1/2 hours
10 – 12 lbs (4.5 – 5.5 kg)	3 – 3 1/4 hours	3 1/2 – 3 3/4 hours
12 – 16 lbs (5.5 – 7 kg)	3 1/4 – 3 1/2 hours	3 3/4 – 4 hours
16 – 22 lbs (7 – 10 kg)	3 1/2 – 4 hours	4 – 4 1/2 hours

* based on a pre-heated 325°F (160°C) standard oven

1. Roast Turkey, page 52
2. Cranberry Sauce, page 55
3. Sausage Stuffing, page 55

Great gravy is so simple to make. Make it in your roasting pan to get all the extra flavour from those brown bits.

Poultry Gravy

Fat from pan drippings	1/4 cup	60 mL
All-purpose flour	1/4 cup	60 mL
Pan drippings (without fat), see Note	2 cups	500 mL

Salt, sprinkle
Pepper, sprinkle

Heat fat from pan drippings in medium saucepan on medium until hot. Add flour. Heat and stir for about 1 minute until bubbling.

Slowly add pan drippings, stirring constantly. Heat and stir for about 10 minutes until boiling and thickened.

Add salt and pepper. Stir. Makes about 2 cups (500 mL).

1/4 cup (60 mL): 76 Calories; 6.7 g Total Fat (2.9 g Mono, 1.6 g Poly, 2.0 g Sat); 7 mg Cholesterol; 3 g Carbohydrate; trace Fibre; 1 g Protein; 371 mg Sodium

Pictured below.

Note: If you don't end up with enough pan drippings, you can add prepared broth, your own poultry stock or water to make 2 cups (500 mL).

Sausage Stuffing

Package of frozen pork sausage meat, thawed	13 oz.	375 g
Chopped celery	1 cup	250 mL
Chopped onion	1 cup	250 mL
Dry white bread cubes	6 cups	1.5 L
Fine dry bread crumbs	2 cups	500 mL
Water	3/4 cup	175 mL
Parsley flakes	1 tbsp.	15 mL
Poultry seasoning	1 tbsp.	15 mL
Salt	1 1/2 tsp.	7 mL
Pepper	1/2 tsp.	2 mL

Scramble-fry first 3 ingredients in large frying pan until sausage is no longer pink.

Combine remaining 7 ingredients in large bowl. Add sausage mixture. Stir until mixture holds together lightly. Makes about 11 cups (2.75 L).

1 cup (250 mL): 227 Calories; 8.7 g Total Fat (3.7 g Mono, 1.4 g Poly, 2.8 g Sat); 28 mg Cholesterol; 27 g Carbohydrate; 1 g Fibre; 9 g Protein; 890 mg Sodium

Pictured on page 53.

This hearty sausage stuffing adds a whole new dimension of flavour to your turkey. This recipe makes enough stuffing for a 12 to 14 lb. (5.4 to 6.3 kg) turkey.

sausage stuffing casserole

For stuffing without the turkey, spread stuffing evenly in a greased 3 quart (3 L) casserole dish, and bake, covered, in a 350°F (175°C) oven for about 45 minutes until heated through.

Cranberry Sauce

Fresh (or frozen) cranberries	2 cups	500 mL
Granulated sugar	1 cup	250 mL
Water	1 cup	250 mL

Combine all 3 ingredients in small saucepan. Bring to a boil. Reduce heat to medium-low. Simmer, uncovered, for about 5 minutes, stirring occasionally, until cranberries split. Remove from heat. Sauce will thicken as it cools. Makes about 2 cups (500 mL).

2 tbsp. (30 mL): 50 Calories; trace Total Fat (0 g Mono, 0 g Poly, 0 g Sat); 0 mg Cholesterol; 13 g Carbohydrate; trace Fibre; trace Protein; trace Sodium

Pictured on front cover and page 53.

Give your can opener a much-deserved holiday, and show off your cooking talents by making your own cranberry sauce. It's simple to do and the results are so impressive.

Serving stuffing in these compact, single-serve portions is a real ball—and you don't need a turkey to cook them! They also go great with roast veal, pork and ham.

make ahead

Assemble these stuffing balls the night before and store, covered, in the fridge until you're ready to bake them.

Stuffing Balls

Butter (or hard margarine)	1/4 cup	60 mL
Chopped celery	1/2 cup	125 mL
Chopped onion	1/2 cup	125 mL
Can of cream-style corn	14 oz.	398 mL
Parsley flakes	2 tsp.	10 mL
Poultry seasoning	1 1/2 tsp.	7 mL
Salt	1 tsp.	5 mL
Pepper	1/4 tsp.	1 mL
Coarse dry bread crumbs	6 cups	1.5 L
Large eggs, fork-beaten	3	3
Butter (or hard margarine), melted	1/2 cup	125 mL

Melt first amount of butter in large frying pan on medium. Add celery and onion. Cook for 5 to 10 minutes, stirring often, until softened.

Add next 5 ingredients. Stir. Bring to a boil. Remove from heat.

Measure bread crumbs into large bowl. Add corn mixture. Stir.

Add eggs. Mix well. Shape into 3 inch (7.5 cm) balls. Arrange in 9 x 13 inch (22 x 33 cm) baking dish.

Pour second amount of butter over balls. Bake, covered, in 350°F (175°C) oven for about 25 minutes until heated through. Makes about 8 stuffing balls.

1 stuffing ball: 539 Calories; 23.4 g Total Fat (6.4 g Mono, 1.7 g Poly, 12.4 g Sat); 126 mg Cholesterol; 70 g Carbohydrate; 3 g Fibre; 14 g Protein; 1284 mg Sodium

Pictured below.

Wild Rice Stuffing

Water	3 cups	750 mL
Chicken bouillon powder	1 tbsp.	15 mL
Long grain brown rice	1/2 cup	125 mL
Wild rice	1/2 cup	125 mL
Butter (or hard margarine)	2 tbsp.	30 mL
Chopped fresh white mushrooms	3 cups	750 mL
Chopped onion	1 cup	250 mL
Chopped celery	1/4 cup	60 mL
Chopped pecans	1/2 cup	125 mL
Parsley flakes	1 tsp.	5 mL
Dried thyme	1/4 tsp.	1 mL
Ground marjoram	1/4 tsp.	1 mL

Combine water and bouillon powder in large saucepan. Bring to a boil. Add brown rice and wild rice. Stir. Reduce heat to medium-low. Simmer, covered, for 45 to 60 minutes, without stirring, until rice is tender. Drain.

Melt butter in large frying pan on medium. Add next 3 ingredients. Cook for about 10 minutes, stirring often, until vegetables are softened and liquid is evaporated.

Add remaining 4 ingredients. Stir. Add to rice mixture. Stir well. Makes about 4 cups (1 L).

1/2 cup (125 mL): 191 Calories; 9.0 g Total Fat (4.0 g Mono, 2.0 g Poly, 2.4 g Sat); 7.8 mg Cholesterol; 24 g Carbohydrate; 2 g Fibre; 5 g Protein; 361 mg Sodium

Pictured on front cover.

Add a little whole-grain goodness to your holiday dinner! This stuffing also goes great with Cornish hens, chicken or salmon.

wild rice stuffing casserole

Have stuffing anytime by spreading the stuffing evenly in a greased 1 1/2 quart (1.5 L) casserole dish. Bake, covered, in a 350°F (175°C) oven for about 30 minutes until heated through.

This delicious roast, complete with stuffing, is a real stunner—and the leftovers make for some fantastic sandwiches!

about serving sizes

The portion sizes for meat in this book are based on Health Canada's recommended serving sizes. That means that each serving of meat will be approximately the size of a deck of cards. So, if you feel the stated serving size is not enough to allow everyone at your table to have larger portions or seconds, we strongly recommend you opt for a larger amount of meat and adjust your recipe accordingly. Of course, a bigger piece of meat will take longer to cook, so it is important that you use a meat thermometer to check for doneness.

Apricot Pork Loin Roast

STUFFING

Water	1/3 cup	75 mL
Fresh spinach leaves, lightly packed	6 cups	1.5 L
White bread cubes	4 cups	1 L
Chopped dried apricot	1 cup	250 mL
Finely chopped onion	1 cup	250 mL
Butter (or hard margarine), melted	1/3 cup	75 mL
Chopped fresh parsley (or 1 tbsp., 15 mL, flakes)	1/4 cup	60 mL
Apricot jam	3 tbsp.	50 mL
Garlic cloves, minced (or 1/2 tsp., 2 mL, powder)	2	2
Salt	1/4 tsp.	1 mL

PORK ROAST

Boneless pork loin roast	5 lbs.	2.3 kg
Dijon mustard (with whole seeds)	1/4 cup	60 mL
Apricot jam	3 tbsp.	50 mL
Dijon mustard (with whole seeds)	2 tbsp.	30 mL

Stuffing: Pour water into medium saucepan. Bring to a boil. Add spinach. Heat and stir until wilted. Drain. Let stand until cool enough to handle. Squeeze dry.

Combine next 8 ingredients in large bowl.

Pork Roast: Cut roast in half lengthwise. Place halves, cut-side up, on work surface. Spread first amount of mustard evenly over cut sides of roast. Spread half of bread mixture over 1 half. Spread spinach over top. Spread remaining bread mixture over spinach. Place other half of roast, mustard-side down, over stuffing. Tie with butcher's string. Place on greased wire rack set in large roasting pan. Bake, uncovered, in 325°F (160°C) oven for 1 hour.

Combine jam and second amount of mustard in small bowl. Spread evenly over roast. Bake for about 1 hour until meat thermometer inserted into thickest part of roast (not stuffing) reads at least 155°F (68°C) or until desired doneness. Remove roast to cutting board. Cover with foil. Let stand for 10 minutes. Cut into 1/2 inch (12 mm) thick slices. Makes 20 servings (2 to 3 oz., 57 to 85 g each, cooked weight).

1 serving: 288 Calories; 15.1 g Total Fat (5.9 g Mono, 1.2 g Poly, 6.3 g Sat); 76 mg Cholesterol; 14 g Carbohydrate; 1 g Fibre; 24 g Protein; 259 mg Sodium

Pictured at right.

Applesauce

Medium peeled cooking apples (such as McIntosh), chopped	4	4
Water	1/2 cup	125 mL
Granulated sugar	1/4 cup	60 mL
Ground cinnamon, just a pinch (optional)		

Combine apple and water in small saucepan. Bring to a boil. Reduce heat to medium-low. Simmer, covered, for about 15 minutes, stirring occasionally, until soft.

Add sugar and cinnamon. Mix well. Makes about 2 cups (500 mL).

1/4 cup (60 mL): 54 Calories; 0.1 g Total Fat (0 g Mono, trace Poly, trace Sat); 0 mg Cholesterol; 14 g Carbohydrate; 1 g Fibre; trace g Protein; trace Sodium

There's no mistaking homemade applesauce for store-bought! Who would have thought it'd be so easy to make?

Apricot Pork Loin Roast, page 58

There's nothing more comforting than succulent roast beef—especially when it's seasoned with Dijon and horseradish. Serve with Creamy Horseradish Sauce, below, on the side.

Comfort Roast

Dijon mustard	3 tbsp.	50 mL
Prepared horseradish	1 tbsp.	15 mL
Garlic clove, minced	1	1
(or 1/4 tsp., 1 mL, powder)		
Montreal steak spice	1 tsp.	5 mL
Beef sirloin tip roast	3 lbs.	1.4 kg

Combine first 4 ingredients in small bowl.

Place roast on large plate. Rub mustard mixture on roast. Let stand, covered, in refrigerator for at least 6 hours or overnight. Place roast on greased wire rack set in 9 x 9 inch (22 x 22 cm) pan. Bake, uncovered, in 475°F (240°C) oven for about 30 minutes until browned. Reduce heat to 300°F (150°C). Bake for another 2 to 2 1/2 hours until meat thermometer inserted into thickest part of roast reads 160°F (71°C) for medium or until desired doneness.
Remove roast to cutting board. Cover with foil. Let stand for 10 minutes.
Slice roast. Makes 12 servings (2 to 3 oz., 57 to 85 g each, cooked weight).

1 serving: 155 Calories; 6.0 g Total Fat (2.4 g Mono, 0.2 g Poly, 2.2 g Sat); 54 mg Cholesterol; trace Carbohydrate; trace Fibre; 23 g Protein; 146 mg Sodium

Pictured at right.

This classic sauce is the perfect complement to roast beef, potatoes, even vegetables.

make ahead

Prepare this revved-up horseradish up to two days in advance and store in an airtight container.

Creamy Horseradish Sauce

Sour cream	1 cup	250 mL
Dijon mustard	1 tbsp.	15 mL
Prepared horseradish	1 tbsp.	15 mL
Lemon juice	1 tsp.	5 mL
Salt	1/4 tsp.	1 mL
Pepper	1/8 tsp.	0.5 mL

Combine all 6 ingredients in small bowl. Makes about 1 cup (250 mL).

2 tbsp. (30 mL): 53 Calories; 5.0 g Total Fat (1.4 g Mono, 0.2 g Poly, 3.1 g Sat); 12 mg Cholesterol; 1 g Carbohydrate; trace Fibre; 1 g Protein; 113 mg Sodium

Pictured at right.

1. Confetti Beans, page 78
2. Creamy Horseradish Sauce, page 60
3. Comfort Roast, page 60

Crispy on the outside, soft and tender on the inside, Yorkshire pudding is the perfect complement to roast beef—and is surprisingly easy to make.

Yorkshire Pudding

All-purpose flour	2 cups	500 mL
Salt	1 tsp.	5 mL
Large eggs	3	3
Milk	1 cup	250 mL
Water	1 cup	250 mL

Combine flour and salt in large bowl.

Add next 3 ingredients. Beat until bubbles start to form around edges of bowl. Let stand, covered, at room temperature for 1 hour. Place muffin pan in 450°F (230°C) oven for about 20 minutes until very hot. Working quickly, remove pan from oven and spray with cooking spray. Fill 12 muffin cups 3/4 full. Bake on centre rack in oven for 15 minutes. Reduce heat to 350°F (175°C). Bake for 15 to 20 minutes until puffed and golden. Makes 12 Yorkshire puddings.

1 Yorkshire pudding: 93 Calories; 1.3 g Total Fat (0.1 g Mono, 0 g Poly, 0.5 g Sat); 55 mg Cholesterol; 16 g Carbohydrate; trace Fibre; 4 g Protein; 222 mg Sodium

Pictured below.

French Tourtière

Lean ground beef	2 lb.	900 g
Lean ground pork	1 lb.	454 g
Water	1 1/2 cups	375 mL
Finely chopped onion	1 1/3 cups	325 mL
Ground allspice	1 tsp.	5 mL
Salt	2 tsp.	10 mL
Pepper	1/2 tsp.	2 mL
Garlic powder	1/2 tsp.	2 mL
Ground cloves	1/8 tsp.	0.5 mL
Fine dry bread crumbs	3/4 cup	175 mL
Pastry for 2 double crust 9 inch (22 cm) pies		

Combine first 9 ingredients in Dutch oven or large pot. Bring to a boil. Reduce heat to medium-low. Simmer, uncovered, for 20 minutes, stirring occasionally.

Add bread crumbs. Stir. Mixture should be moist and thick. Cool.

Divide pastry into 4 portions, making 2 portions slightly larger than the others. Shape each portion into slightly flattened disc. Roll out 2 larger portions, 1 at a time, on lightly floured surface to about 1/8 inch (3 mm) thickness. Line two 9 inch (22 cm) pie plates. Spoon meat mixture into shells. Roll out remaining 2 pastry portions, 1 at a time, on lightly floured surface to about 1/8 inch (3 mm) thickness. Dampen edges of shells with water. Cover meat mixture with pastry. Trim and crimp decorative edges to seal. Cut several small vents in tops to allow steam to escape. Bake on bottom rack in 375°F (190°C) oven for about 1 hour until golden. Each pie cuts into 8 wedges, for a total of 16 wedges.

1 serving: 338 Calories; 21.1 g Total Fat (6.3 g Mono, 0.8 g Poly, 8.4 g Sat); 59 mg Cholesterol; 18 g Carbohydrate; trace Fibre; 18 g Protein; 488 mg Sodium

Enjoy this French-Canadian Christmas favourite of seasoned ground meat pie. Make in advance and freeze to free up your time during the holiday rush.

about tourtière

For Catholic French Canadians, Christmas Eve is when most of the holiday festivities take place. Celebrations begin in the evening with a party or a special meal and gift opening. This is then followed by Midnight Mass. Upon returning home from church, the *réveillon*, a festive meal, begins and tourtière is served. Traditionally made with ground pork, tourtière can also be made with ground beef or a combination of ground meats.

Coulibiac (koo-lee-BYAHK), a salmon, rice and mushroom-stuffed pastry, always makes a delicious holiday treat. Serve with Egg And Parsley Sauce, page 66.

The origins of Rudolph the Red-Nosed Reindeer are quite unique. He didn't begin life as a story or a song, he began life as an advertising campaign! His first appearance was in 1939 in illustrated poem format as a promotional giveaway for the Montgomery Ward department store in Chicago. It wasn't until 1947 that the Christmas song was written, and it took two more years before anyone agreed to sing it! In 1949, Gene Autry recorded the now famous song, and the character of Rudolph became a sensation on an international scope. The very popular claymation television special wasn't created until 1964.

Coulibiac

FILLING

Butter (or hard margarine)	1 tbsp.	15 mL
Sliced fresh white mushrooms	2 cups	500 mL
Chopped onion	1/2 cup	125 mL
Package of puff pastry, thawed according to package directions	14 oz.	397 g
Cooked long grain and wild rice mix	1 1/4 cups	300 mL
Sour cream	1 cup	250 mL
Large hard-cooked eggs, coarsely chopped	4	4
Chopped fresh dill (or 3/4 tsp., 4 mL, dried)	1 tbsp.	15 mL
Chopped fresh chives (or 1/2 tsp., 2 mL, dried)	2 tsp.	10 mL
Fresh (or frozen, thawed) salmon fillet (tail end), skin removed	1 1/2 lbs.	680 g
Salt, sprinkle		
Pepper, sprinkle		
Large egg	1	1
Water	1 tbsp.	15 mL

Filling: Melt butter in large frying pan on medium. Add mushrooms and onion. Cook for 8 to 10 minutes, stirring often, until onion is softened and liquid is evaporated. Transfer to large bowl. Cool.

Roll out pastry on lightly floured surface to 8 inches (20 cm) wider and 2 inches (5 cm) longer than fillet.

Add rice and sour cream to mushroom mixture. Mix well. Spread evenly down centre of pastry.

Sprinkle next 3 ingredients over rice mixture. Place fillet on top. Sprinkle with salt and pepper.

(continued on next page)

Beat egg and water in small bowl until smooth. Brush on long edges of pastry. Bring the long edges together at centre. Pinch edges together, folding to create package. Place, seam-side down, on ungreased baking sheet, tucking ends underneath package to seal. Brush with remaining egg mixture. Cut several small vents in top to allow steam to escape. Bake in 400°F (205°C) oven for about 30 minutes until golden. Let stand for 10 minutes before serving. Serves 8.

1 serving: 604 Calories; 38.3 g Total Fat (10.6 g Mono, 15.0 g Poly, 9.7 g Sat); 199 mg Cholesterol; 37 g Carbohydrate; 1 g Fibre; 27 g Protein; 444 mg Sodium

Pictured below.

Coulibiac, page 64, with
Egg And Parsley Sauce, page 66

This multipurpose sauce is great with Coulibiac, page 64, and other fish dishes, or poured over steamed cauliflower and broccoli.

Egg And Parsley Sauce

Butter (or hard margarine)	2 tbsp.	30 mL
Finely chopped onion	1/4 cup	60 mL
All-purpose flour	2 tbsp.	30 mL
Half-and-half cream (or homogenized milk)	1 cup	250 mL
Milk	1 cup	250 mL
Salt, sprinkle		
Pepper, sprinkle		
Large hard-cooked eggs, finely chopped	2	2
Finely chopped fresh parsley	1 tbsp.	15 mL
(or 3/4 tsp., 4 mL, flakes)		

Melt butter in medium saucepan on medium. Add onion. Cook, uncovered, for about 5 minutes, stirring often, until softened.

Add flour. Heat and stir for 1 minute.

Slowly add cream and milk, stirring constantly, until smooth. Heat and stir for about 3 minutes until boiling and thickened. Add salt and pepper. Stir. Remove from heat.

Add egg and parsley. Stir until heated through. Makes about 2 1/4 cups (550 mL).

2 tbsp. (30 mL): 45 Calories; 3.3 g Total Fat (1.0 g Mono, 0.2 g Poly, 1.9 g Sat); 31 mg Cholesterol; 2 g Carbohydrate; trace Fibre; 2 g Protein; 28 mg Sodium

Pictured on page 65.

Triple Seafood Noodles

Water	12 cups	3 L
Salt	1 1/2 tsp.	7 mL
Medium egg noodles	7 1/2 cups	1.9 L
Butter (or hard margarine)	3 tbsp.	50 mL
Sliced fresh white mushrooms	4 cups	1 L
Can of diced tomatoes (with juice)	14 oz.	398 mL
Dry (or alcohol-free) white wine	1/4 cup	60 mL
Vegetable (or chicken) bouillon powder	1 tbsp.	15 mL
Dried basil	2 tsp.	10 mL
Parsley flakes	1 tsp.	5 mL
Garlic powder	1/2 tsp.	2 mL
Butter (or hard margarine)	3 tbsp.	50 mL
Can of frozen lobster meat, thawed and drained, cut up	11.3 oz.	320 g
Can of crabmeat, drained, cartilage removed, flaked	4 1/4 oz.	120 g
Can of small shrimp, drained (see Note)	4 oz.	106 g
Sliced green onion	1/4 cup	60 mL

Combine water and salt in Dutch oven. Bring to a boil. Add noodles. Boil, uncovered, for 5 to 7 minutes, stirring occasionally, until tender but firm. Drain. Transfer to medium bowl. Cover to keep warm.

Melt first amount of butter in large frying pan on medium-high. Add mushrooms. Cook for about 5 minutes, stirring occasionally, until softened and starting to turn golden.

Combine next 6 ingredients in same Dutch oven. Heat and stir on medium until boiling. Add mushrooms. Simmer, uncovered, for 3 minutes to blend flavours. Cover to keep warm.

Melt second amount of butter in same frying pan on medium. Add remaining 4 ingredients. Cook and stir until heated through. Add to tomato mixture. Add noodles. Toss. Makes about 13 cups (3.25 L).

1 cup (250 mL): 186 Calories; 6.6 g Total Fat (1.7 g Mono, 0.6 g Poly, 3.6 g Sat); 71 mg Cholesterol; 18 g Carbohydrate; 1 g Fibre; 12 g Protein; 581 mg Sodium

Note: If you prefer cooked salad shrimp, use 3/4 cup (175 mL) instead of a 4 oz. (106 g) can of small shrimp.

We certainly believe there's no such thing as too much turkey, but if you desire a little variety, this delightful and extravagant seafood medley is just the thing for an elegant holiday dinner party. If you can't find frozen canned lobster in your grocery store, you'll find it in a fish market.

christmas fun

Which came first, the story or the song? In the case of *Frosty the Snowman*, it was definitely the song. Written in 1950, the song was first popularized by singing cowboy Gene Autry. It wasn't until almost 20 years later that the animated film, narrated by Jimmy Durante, was made.

Glazed Parsnips

Parsnips, cut into bite-sized pieces	1 lb.	454 g
Brown sugar, packed	1/4 cup	60 mL
Orange juice	3 tbsp.	50 mL
Butter (or hard margarine)	2 tbsp.	30 mL

Pour water into medium saucepan until about 1 inch (2.5 cm) deep. Add parsnip. Cover. Bring to a boil. Reduce heat to medium. Boil gently for about 10 minutes until tender-crisp. Drain. Transfer to serving bowl.

Combine remaining 3 ingredients in small saucepan. Heat and stir on medium until boiling. Pour over parsnip. Toss until coated. Serves 4.

1 serving: 192 Calories; 6.1 g Total Fat (1.6 g Mono, 0.3 g Poly, 3.7 g Sat); 15 mg Cholesterol; 35 g Carbohydrate; 4 g Fibre; 2 g Protein; 57 mg Sodium

Potatoes Extraordinaire

Peeled potatoes, cut up	5 lbs.	2.3 kg
Block of cream cheese, cut up and softened	8 oz.	250 g
Sour cream	1 cup	250 mL
Butter (or hard margarine), softened	1/4 cup	60 mL
Onion salt	1 tbsp.	15 mL
Salt	1 tsp.	5 mL
Pepper	1/4 tsp.	1 mL
Butter (or hard margarine), softened	2 tbsp.	30 mL
Paprika, sprinkle		

Pour water into Dutch oven or large pot until about 1 inch (2.5 cm) deep. Add potato. Cover. Bring to a boil. Reduce heat to medium. Boil gently for 12 to 15 minutes until tender. Drain. Mash.

Add cream cheese, a few pieces at a time, stirring constantly, until melted. Add next 5 ingredients. Beat until smooth and fluffy. Transfer to greased 3 quart (3 L) casserole.

(continued on next page)

Spoon dabs of second amount of butter, using 1/2 tsp. (2 mL) for each, over potatoes. Sprinkle with paprika. Bake, covered, in 350°F (175°C) oven until heated through. Serves 12.

1 serving: 315 Calories; 15.9 g Total Fat (4.3 g Mono, 0.7 g Poly, 9.9 g Sat); 44 mg Cholesterol; 39 g Carbohydrate; 3 g Fibre; 5 g Protein; 760 mg Sodium

Pictured below.

Top: Potatoes Extraordinaire, page 68
Bottom: Festive Scalloped Potatoes, page 70

When the mercury drops below zero, scalloped potatoes become a winter necessity. This version is festive because the red onion adds a nice splash of colour.

christmas fun

According to German mythology, nutcrackers, the little wooden or metal soldier dolls, are said to protect a house from evil spirits. Often nutcrackers are depicted with their teeth bared and a scowl—all the better to intimidate any intruders! After all, who would mess with a little fellow who cracks walnuts with his teeth?

Festive Scalloped Potatoes

Butter (or hard margarine)	1/2 cup	125 mL
All-purpose flour	1/2 cup	125 mL
Salt	2 tsp.	10 mL
Pepper	1/2 tsp.	2 mL
Paprika	1/2 tsp.	2 mL
Milk	4 1/2 cups	1.1 L
Medium peeled potatoes, thinly sliced	8	8
Medium red (or white) onion, thinly sliced, rings separated	1	1
Paprika, sprinkle		

Melt butter in small saucepan on medium. Add next 4 ingredients. Heat and stir for 1 minute.

Slowly add milk, stirring constantly, with whisk. Heat and stir until boiling and thickened.

To assemble, layer ingredients in greased 3 quart (3 L) casserole as follows:

1. Half of potato
2. Half of onion rings
3. Half of milk mixture
4. Remaining potato
5. Remaining onion rings
6. Remaining milk mixture

Sprinkle paprika over top. Bake, covered, in 350°F (175°C) oven for 1 hour. Bake, uncovered, for about 10 minutes until golden and potatoes are tender. Serves 8.

1 serving: 294 Calories; 12.8 g Total Fat (3.5 g Mono, 0.4 g Poly, 8.0 g Sat); 39 mg Cholesterol; 40 g Carbohydrate; 3 g Fibre; 10 g Protein; 739 mg Sodium

Pictured on page 69.

Barley And Rice Pilaf

Olive (or cooking) oil	1 tbsp.	15 mL
Chopped celery	1 cup	250 mL
Chopped onion	1 cup	250 mL
Garlic cloves, minced	2	2
(or 1/2 tsp., 2 mL, powder)		
Olive (or cooking) oil	1 tbsp.	15 mL
Pearl barley	1 1/4 cups	300 mL
Long grain brown rice	1 cup	250 mL
Boiling water	6 cups	1.5 L
Julienned carrot (see Tip)	1 cup	250 mL
Chicken (or vegetable) bouillon powder	3 tbsp.	50 mL
Parsley flakes	1 tbsp.	15 mL
Dried crushed chilies (optional)	1/4 tsp.	1 mL

Heat first amount of olive oil in large frying pan on medium. Add next 3 ingredients. Cook for 5 to 10 minutes, stirring often, until onion is softened. Transfer to ungreased 3 quart (3 L) casserole.

Heat second amount of olive oil in same frying pan. Add barley and rice. Heat and stir for about 5 minutes until starting to turn golden. Add to onion mixture.

Add remaining 5 ingredients. Stir. Bake, covered, in 350°F (175°C) oven for about 2 hours until barley is tender and liquid is absorbed. Fluff with fork. Makes about 9 1/2 cups (2.4 L).

1 cup (250 mL): 101 Calories; 3.8 g Total Fat (2.4 g Mono, 0.6 g Poly, 0.6 g Sat); 1 mg Cholesterol; 15 g Carbohydrate; 2 g Fibre; 2 g Protein; 854 mg Sodium

Pictured below.

Instead of serving the mashed potatoes that everyone has come to expect, treat your guests to this hearty pilaf.

tip

To julienne, cut into very thin strips that resemble matchsticks.

Traditional Brussels sprouts are made even more delicious with sweet peas, smoky bacon and earthy pine nuts.

Sweet And Smoky Brussels Sprouts

Bacon slices, diced	4	4
Finely chopped onion	1 cup	250 mL
Brussels sprouts (about 3 lbs., 1.4 kg), trimmed and halved lengthwise	12 cups	3 L
Prepared chicken broth	1 1/4 cups	300 mL
Frozen peas	2 cups	500 mL
Pine nuts, toasted (see Tip)	2/3 cup	150 mL
Grated Parmesan cheese	1/3 cup	75 mL
Butter (or hard margarine)	1 tbsp.	15 mL

Cook bacon in Dutch oven or large pot on medium until crisp. Transfer with slotted spoon to paper towels to drain. Set aside.

Heat 2 tsp. (10 mL) drippings in same Dutch oven on medium. Add onion. Cook for 5 to 10 minutes, stirring often, until softened.

Add Brussels sprouts and broth. Bring to a boil. Reduce heat to medium. Boil gently, covered, for about 10 minutes until Brussels sprouts are tender-crisp.

Add peas and bacon. Stir. Cook, covered, for about 2 minutes until heated through and peas are tender.

Add remaining 3 ingredients. Heat and stir until butter is melted. Makes about 11 cups (2.75 L).

1 cup (250 mL): 244 Calories; 13.1 g Total Fat (4.5 g Mono, 2.9 g Poly, 5.1 g Sat); 17 mg Cholesterol; 22 g Carbohydrate; 9 g Fibre; 15 g Protein; 562 mg Sodium

Pictured at right.

This cheesy, savoury casserole with a golden crumb topping really "turns-up" the flavour!

Turnip Cheese Casserole

Block of cream cheese, softened	4 oz.	125 g
Mashed yellow turnip	3 cups	750 mL
Butter (or hard margarine), softened	1/4 cup	60 mL
Brown sugar, packed	2 tbsp.	30 mL
Salt, sprinkle		
Pepper, sprinkle		
Butter (or hard margarine)	1 tbsp.	15 mL
Fine dry bread crumbs	1/4 cup	60 mL

Mash cream cheese with fork in large bowl. Add next 5 ingredients. Mix well. Transfer to greased 2 quart (2 L) shallow baking dish.

Melt second amount of butter in small saucepan on medium. Remove from heat. Add bread crumbs. Stir well. Sprinkle over turnip mixture. Bake, uncovered, in 350°F (175°C) oven for 15 to 20 minutes until heated through. Serves 8.

1 serving: 157 Calories; 12.3 g Total Fat (3.3 g Mono, 0.5 g Poly, 7.7 g Sat); 34 mg Cholesterol; 11 g Carbohydrate; 2 g Fibre; 2 g Protein; 370 mg Sodium

Anyone with a sweet tooth will delight over these marmalade and brown sugar-coated beauties.

Marmalade-Glazed Sweet Potatoes

Peeled sweet potatoes, cut into bite-sized pieces	3 lbs.	1.4 kg
Cooking oil	1 1/2 tbsp.	25 mL
Salt	1 tsp.	5 mL
Coarsely ground pepper	1 tsp.	5 mL
Marmalade	1/4 cup	60 mL
Butter (or hard margarine), melted	3 tbsp.	50 mL
Brown sugar, packed	2 tbsp.	30 mL

Put first 4 ingredients into large bowl. Toss until coated. Arrange in single layer on ungreased baking sheet with sides. Bake in 325°F (160°C) oven for 30 minutes.

Combine remaining 3 ingredients in small bowl. Drizzle over sweet potato. Toss until coated. Bake for another 15 minutes until sweet potato is tender. Serves 8.

1 serving: 299 Calories; 7.1 g Total Fat (2.6 g Mono, 1.1 g Poly, 2.9 g Sat); 11 mg Cholesterol; 58 g Carbohydrate; 7 g Fibre; 3 g Protein; 345 mg Sodium

Pictured on front cover.

Sweet Potato Casserole

Large eggs, fork-beaten	2	2
Mashed sweet potatoes	3 cups	750 mL
Butter (or hard margarine), softened	1/4 cup	60 mL
Granulated sugar	1/4 cup	60 mL
Vanilla extract	1 tsp.	5 mL
Salt	1/4 tsp.	1 mL
Butter (or hard margarine)	1/4 cup	60 mL
Brown sugar, packed	1/2 cup	125 mL
Chopped pecans	1/2 cup	125 mL
All-purpose flour	1/4 cup	60 mL

The sweetness in this brown sugar-accented casserole is the perfect contrast for all those savoury Christmas supper staples.

Combine first 6 ingredients in medium bowl. Transfer to greased 2 quart (2 L) shallow baking dish.

Melt second amount of butter in small saucepan on medium. Remove from heat. Add remaining 3 ingredients. Stir well. Sprinkle over sweet potato mixture. Bake, uncovered, in 350°F (175°C) oven for about 30 minutes until golden. Serves 8.

1 serving: 325 Calories; 17.9 g Total Fat (5.9 g Mono, 2.1 g Poly, 8.1 g Sat); 84 mg Cholesterol; 39 g Carbohydrate; 3 g Fibre; 4 g Protein; 360 mg Sodium

Pictured below.

The scent of cinnamon is so reminiscent of a cozy Christmas. Use this scent memory to your advantage and serve this aromatic side that's sure to put all in a holiday mood.

make your own cinnamon honey

Combine 1/2 cup (125 mL) of liquid honey and 1/4 tsp. (1 mL) ground cinnamon and, *voila*, your honey's even sweeter!

Cinnamon Honey Carrots

Bags of baby carrots (2 lbs., 900 g, each)	**2**	**2**
Butter (or hard margarine)	1/2 cup	125 mL
Cinnamon honey	1/2 cup	125 mL
Chopped fresh parsley	1/3 cup	75 mL

Pour water into large saucepan until about 1 inch (2.5 cm) deep. Add carrots. Cover. Bring to a boil. Reduce heat to medium. Boil gently for about 8 minutes until tender-crisp. Drain. Transfer to medium bowl. Cover to keep warm.

Combine remaining 3 ingredients in same saucepan. Cook on medium for about 5 minutes, stirring occasionally, until boiling and slightly thickened. Add carrots. Heat and stir for about 3 minutes until carrots are coated and heated through. Serves 12.

1 serving: 170 Calories; 8.4 g Total Fat (2.0 g Mono, 0.7 g Poly, 4.9 g Sat); 20 mg Cholesterol; 24 g Carbohydrate; 3 g Fibre; 1 g Protein; 108 mg Sodium

Pictured at right.

This quick and easy casserole is perfect for the busy holiday season.

fresh broccoli casserole

If you prefer fresh veggies in your casserole, use 6 cups (1.5 L) of fresh broccoli instead of frozen. Blanch the broccoli in boiling water in a large saucepan for about 5 minutes until bright green. Drain and transfer to the casserole dish. Add the soup mixture and top with the onions. Bake, as directed, until bubbly and hot.

Broccoli Casserole

Can of condensed cream of mushroom soup	10 oz.	284 mL
Process cheese spread	1/2 cup	125 mL
Frozen chopped broccoli	6 cups	1.5 L
Can of French-fried onions	2 3/4 oz.	79 g

Beat soup and cheese spread in small bowl until combined.

Arrange broccoli in ungreased 2 quart (2 L) shallow baking dish. Pour soup mixture over top. Bake, uncovered, in 350°F (175°C) oven for about 45 minutes until tender.

Sprinkle onions over top. Bake for 10 minutes. Serves 8.

1 serving: 119 Calories; 10.9 g Total Fat (trace Mono, 0.2 g Poly, 4.7 g Sat); 14 mg Cholesterol; 16 g Carbohydrate; 4 g Fibre; 7 g Protein; 653 mg Sodium

Pictured at right.

Top: Broccoli Casserole, above
Bottom: Cinnamon Honey Carrots, above

Add some colour to your dinner table. Ordinary green beans get a festive makeover with vibrant flecks of red and yellow pepper.

make ahead

Get the most time-consuming prep jobs out of the way up to eight hours in advance. Trim the beans, dice the peppers and store in separate containers in the fridge.

These dressed-up beets are sure to impress all your nearest and dearest this holiday season.

time-saving tip

Put that vegetable scrubber away! Use one 14 oz. (398 mL) can of beets instead of fresh beets. Heat, with liquid, in a small saucepan until heated through. Add orange juice mixture and stir until coated.

Confetti Beans

Fresh (or frozen) whole green beans	4 cups	1 L
Butter (or hard margarine)	2 tbsp.	30 mL
Finely diced red pepper	1/4 cup	60 mL
Finely diced yellow pepper	1/4 cup	60 mL
Finely chopped fresh chives	2 tbsp.	30 mL

Pour water into large saucepan until about 1 inch (2.5 cm) deep. Add green beans. Cover. Bring to a boil. Reduce heat to medium. Boil gently for about 5 minutes until tender-crisp. Drain.

Melt butter in large frying pan on medium. Add red pepper, yellow pepper and green beans. Heat and stir for 2 to 3 minutes until peppers are softened. Transfer to serving bowl.

Sprinkle chives over top. Makes about 4 cups (1 L).

1 cup (250 mL): 81 Calories; 5.7 g Total Fat (1.5 g Mono, 0.2 g Poly, 3.6 g Sat); 15 mg Cholesterol; 6 g Carbohydrate; 2 g Fibre; 1 g Protein; 131 mg Sodium

Pictured on front cover and pages 61 and 79.

Orange-Sauced Beets

Diced fresh beets	2 cups	500 mL
Orange juice	1/3 cup	75 mL
Brown sugar, packed	1 tbsp.	15 mL
Lemon juice	1 1/2 tsp.	7 mL
Cornstarch	1 tsp.	5 mL
Salt	1/8 tsp.	0.5 mL

Pour water into small saucepan until about 1 inch (2.5 cm) deep. Add beets. Cover. Bring to a boil. Reduce heat to medium. Boil gently for 10 to 15 minutes until tender. Drain. Transfer to serving bowl. Cover to keep warm.

Whisk remaining 5 ingredients in same saucepan. Heat and stir on medium until boiling and thickened. Pour over beets. Toss until coated. Serves 4.

1 serving: 62 Calories; 0.2 g Total Fat (trace Mono, 0.1 g Poly, trace Sat); 0 mg Cholesterol; 15 g Carbohydrate; 2 g Fibre; 2 g Protein; 141 mg Sodium

Pictured at right.

Top: Confetti Beans, above
Bottom: Orange-Sauced Beets, above

This holiday staple is tradition for many families with Ukrainian roots. And although a tad time-consuming, the effort is always appreciated.

Cabbage Rolls

Large head of green cabbage (about 5 lbs., 2.3 kg)	1	1
Boiling water, to cover		
Water	2 1/4 cups	550 mL
Short grain white rice	1 1/2 cups	375 mL
Salt	1 1/2 tsp.	7 mL
Pepper	1/2 tsp.	2 mL
Bacon slices, diced	6	6
Finely chopped onion	2 cups	500 mL
Tomato juice	1 cup	250 mL
Water	2/3 cup	150 mL
Butter (or hard margarine)	1 tbsp.	15 mL

Remove core from cabbage. Trim about 1/2 inch (12 mm) slice from bottom. Place, cut-side down, in Dutch oven or large pot. Cover with boiling water. Cover Dutch oven with foil. Heat on medium-low for about 30 minutes, using tongs to remove leaves to tea towel as they start to soften and loosen. Blot dry. Cut 'V' shape along tough ribs of leaves to remove. Discard ribs. Cut larger leaves into 2 equal pieces. Set aside.

Measure water into medium saucepan. Bring to a boil. Add next 3 ingredients. Stir. Reduce heat to medium-low. Simmer, covered, for about 10 minutes, without stirring, until liquid is absorbed but rice is still firm. Transfer to large bowl. Fluff with fork. Cool.

Cook bacon in large frying pan on medium for about 10 minutes until starting to brown.

Add onion. Cook for about 10 minutes, stirring often, until onion is very soft. Add to rice. Mix well. Spoon about 1 1/2 tbsp. (25 mL) rice mixture onto centre of 1 cabbage leaf. Fold sides over filling. Roll up tightly from bottom to enclose. Repeat with remaining cabbage leaves and rice mixture. Arrange cabbage rolls tightly together, seam-side down, in layers in greased large roasting pan. Layer any remaining cabbage leaves on top of rolls.

(continued on next page)

Combine remaining 3 ingredients in small saucepan. Heat and stir on medium until hot. Pour over cabbage rolls. Bake, covered, in 350°F (175°C) oven for about 1 1/2 hours until liquid is absorbed and cabbage rolls are tender. Makes about 60 cabbage rolls.

1 cabbage roll: 33 Calories; 1.2 g Total Fat (0.8 g Mono, 0.2 g Poly, 0.7 g Sat); 2 mg Cholesterol; 4 g Carbohydrate; 1 g Fibre; 1 g Protein; 98 mg Sodium

Pictured below.

This popular Ukrainian and Polish dish of cheesy, potato-filled dumplings smothered in onion butter is also known as pyrohy, perogies or potato dumplings.

bacon varenyky

Infuse your varenyky with the smoky taste of bacon by adding six bacon slices, cooked crisp and crumbled, to the filling.

fried varenyky

Cook boiled varenyky in small batches in a frying pan with 2 tsp. (10 mL) butter until lightly browned.

Varenyky With Onion Butter

DOUGH		
All-purpose flour	2 cups	500 mL
Salt	1 tsp.	5 mL
Baking powder	1/4 tsp.	1 mL
Cooking oil	2 tsp.	10 mL
Warm water, approximately	2/3 cup	150 mL
ONION BUTTER		
Butter	1/4 cup	60 mL
Finely diced onion	1/2 cup	125 mL
FILLING		
2% cottage cheese	1/3 cup	75 mL
Hot mashed potatoes	1 3/4 cups	425 mL
Grated sharp Cheddar cheese	3/4 cup	175 mL
Pepper	1/8 tsp.	0.5 mL
Water	16 cups	4 L
Salt	2 tsp.	10 mL

Dough: Put first 3 ingredients into food processor. Process until combined.

With motor running, slowly add cooking oil and enough warm water through hole in feed chute until a ball starts to form. Turn out onto lightly floured surface. Knead 3 to 4 times until smooth. Wrap with plastic wrap. Let stand for 20 minutes.

Onion Butter: Melt butter in small saucepan on medium-low. Add onion. Cook for about 10 minutes, stirring often, until onion is soft but not browned. Cover to keep warm.

Filling: Put cottage cheese into medium bowl. Mash with fork to break up any clumps. Add next 3 ingredients. Stir until Cheddar cheese is melted. Divide dough into 4 equal portions. Roll 1 portion into 12 inch (30 cm) long rope. Wrap remaining portions with plastic wrap. Cut rope into 1 inch (2.5 cm) pieces. Shape into balls. Press balls slightly to flatten. Cover with tea towel to prevent drying. Stretch and press 1 ball to about 2 1/2 inch (6.4 cm) diameter circle. Place about 2 tsp. (10 mL) filling in centre. Fold dough over filling. Pinch edges firmly together to seal (see Note 1). Arrange in single layer on waxed paper-lined baking sheet with sides. Cover with separate tea towel to prevent drying. Repeat with remaining dough and filling.

(continued on next page)

Combine water and salt in Dutch oven or large pot. Bring to a boil. Cook varenyky (see Note 2), in batches, for 3 to 4 minutes, stirring occasionally, until varenyky float to top. Cook for 1 minute before removing with slotted spoon to sieve. Drain. Transfer to large bowl. Drizzle with Onion Butter. Gently shake until coated. Cover to keep warm. Makes about 48 varenyky.

1 varenyk: 43 Calories; 1.9 g Total Fat (0.6 g Mono, 0.1 g Poly, 1.1 g Sat); 5 mg Cholesterol; 5 g Carbohydrate; trace Fibre; 1 g Protein; 94 mg Sodium

Pictured below.

Note 1: Edges of dough may be moistened with water, if necessary, to seal.

Note 2: Varenyky freeze well. Just arrange filled varenyky (cooked or uncooked) in layers between sheets of waxed or parchment paper on baking sheet with sides. Cover. Freeze until firm. Store in resealable freezer bags in freezer. Cook as directed, from frozen, but increase cooking time to 5 minutes after varenyky float to top.

This true-to-tradition recipe makes one of the best puddings around. Its light texture pairs magnificently with warm Rum Sauce, page 86. You'll be able to find beef suet in your grocer's meat freezer or at the local butcher's.

about steamed pudding containers

Better known in England and Australia, where steamed puddings are more commonly enjoyed, a pudding container or mold is a metal vessel with a metal lid that is clamped down. Some containers come in various decorative patterns, much like jelly molds. The container itself needs to be placed in a larger pot with water for steaming. Buying pudding containers in Canada can be a bit tricky—you'll most likely have to order one from a specialty store or do some international online shopping.

Steamed Fruit Pudding

All-purpose flour	2 cups	500 mL
Ground beef suet	2 cups	500 mL
Brown sugar, packed	3/4 cup	175 mL
Ground cinnamon	2 tsp.	10 mL
Baking soda	1 tsp.	5 mL
Cream of tartar	1 tsp.	5 mL
Ground cloves	1 tsp.	5 mL
Salt	1 tsp.	5 mL
Large eggs, fork-beaten	2	2
Milk	1 1/4 cups	300 mL
Currants	1 cup	250 mL
Sultana raisins	1 cup	250 mL
Diced mixed peel, finely chopped	3/4 cup	175 mL
Golden raisins	1/2 cup	125 mL

Combine first 8 ingredients in large bowl.

Combine remaining 6 ingredients in medium bowl. Add to flour mixture. Mix. Transfer to greased 2 quart (2 L) pudding container or heatproof bowl. Cover with greased foil, tying down sides with butcher's string. Place in steamer or large pot. Carefully pour enough boiling water into steamer until water comes halfway up side of pudding container. Steam, covered, on medium-low for 4 hours, adding more boiling water as needed to maintain water level. Remove container from steamer. Let stand on wire rack for 30 minutes. Loosen pudding from container and invert onto wire rack. Serves 12.

1 serving: 533 Calories; 37.0 g Total Fat (12.2 g Mono, 1.3 g Poly, 20.4 g Sat); 63 mg Cholesterol; 47 g Carbohydrate; 3 g Fibre; 5 g Protein; 341 mg Sodium

Pictured at right.

Steamed Fruit Pudding, above, with Rum Sauce, page 86

This sweet sauce adds an extra festive touch to Steamed Fruit Pudding, page 84.

Rum Sauce

Butter (or hard margarine)	3 tbsp.	50 mL
All-purpose flour	3 tbsp.	50 mL
Salt	1/2 tsp.	2 mL
Water	1 1/2 cups	375 mL
Brown sugar, packed	3/4 cup	175 mL
Rum extract	1 tsp.	5 mL

Melt butter in small saucepan on medium. Add flour and salt. Heat and stir for 1 minute.

Slowly add water, stirring constantly with whisk, until boiling and thickened.

Add brown sugar and extract. Heat and stir until brown sugar is dissolved. Makes about 2 cups (500 mL).

2 tbsp. (30 mL): 60 Calories; 2.0 g Total Fat (0.5 g Mono, 0.1 g Poly, 1.3 g Sat); 5 mg Cholesterol; 11 g Carbohydrate; trace Fibre; trace Protein; 88 mg Sodium

Pictured on page 85.

Everyone loves the homey and traditional taste of gently spiced bread pudding. If you'd rather, use raisins instead of currants. Great served with Rum Sauce, above, or Vanilla Sauce, page 87.

Raisin Bread Pudding

Can of skim evaporated milk	13 1/2 oz.	385 mL
Milk	1/4 cup	60 mL
Raisin bread slices, cubed	5	5
Butter (or hard margarine)	2 tbsp.	30 mL
Large eggs, fork-beaten	2	2
Brown sugar, packed	2/3 cup	150 mL
Vanilla extract	1 tsp.	5 mL
Salt	1/2 tsp.	2 mL
Currants	1/2 cup	125 mL
Ground cinnamon	1/4 tsp.	1 mL

Combine evaporated milk and milk in large heavy saucepan. Heat and stir on medium until hot, but not boiling. Remove from heat.

Add bread cubes and butter. Stir.

(continued on next page)

Combine next 4 ingredients in small bowl. Add currants and cinnamon. Stir. Add to milk mixture. Stir well. Spread evenly in greased 1 1/2 quart (1.5 L) shallow baking dish. Bake, uncovered, in 350°F (175°C) oven for 40 to 45 minutes until set and knife inserted in centre comes out clean. Serves 6.

1 serving: 276 Calories; 6.5 g Total Fat (1.6 g Mono, 0.3 g Poly, 3.3 g Sat); 85 mg Cholesterol; 46 g Carbohydrate; 1 g Fibre; 10 g Protein; 426 mg Sodium

Pictured below.

Vanilla Sauce

Granulated sugar	1 cup	250 mL
All-purpose flour	3 tbsp.	50 mL
Salt	1/2 tsp.	2 mL
Hot water	1 1/2 cups	375 mL
Butter (or hard margarine)	2 tbsp.	30 mL
Vanilla extract	1 tsp.	5 mL

This sauce adds a glistening touch to pudding, pound cake or fresh fruit.

Combine first 3 ingredients in small saucepan.

Add remaining 3 ingredients. Heat and stir on medium for about 5 minutes until boiling and thickened. Makes about 2 cups (500 mL).

2 tbsp. (30 mL): 62 Calories; 1.4 g Total Fat (0.3 g Mono, 0.1 g Poly, 0.9 g Sat); 4 mg Cholesterol; 13 g Carbohydrate; trace Fibre; trace Protein; 80 mg Sodium

Pictured below.

Raisin Bread Pudding, page 86, with Vanilla Sauce, above

Your regular cream-filled cake dons its holiday apparel in the costume of a yule log. Delicious and fun!

history of the yule log

The tradition of the yule log originated in Germany but quickly spread throughout Europe and North America. How the log is collected varies from region to region, but the lighting of it is meant to be carried out with much pomp and circumstance. The burning of the log symbolizes good luck coming into the home and bad luck going out. Often ashes or splinters are kept as good-luck tokens for the rest of the year.

Chocolate Roulade Yule Log

Egg whites (large), room temperature	6	6
Cream of tartar	1/2 tsp.	2 mL
Egg yolks (large)	6	6
Granulated sugar	1 cup	250 mL
Cocoa, sifted if lumpy	1/3 cup	75 mL
Vanilla extract	1 tsp.	5 mL
Salt, just a pinch		
Cocoa, sifted if lumpy	1/4 cup	60 mL
FILLING		
Whipping cream	2 cups	500 mL
Cocoa, sifted if lumpy	1/2 cup	125 mL
Granulated sugar	1/2 cup	125 mL
Chocolate (or coffee-flavoured) liqueur	1/4 cup	60 mL
Large marshmallow	1	1
Pecan halves	6	6

Line bottom of greased 10 × 15 inch (25 × 38 cm) jelly roll pan with waxed paper. Beat egg whites in large bowl until soft peaks form. Add cream of tartar. Beat until stiff peaks form.

Using same beaters, beat next 5 ingredients in medium bowl for about 2 minutes until thick. Fold in egg whites until no white streaks remain. Pour batter into prepared pan. Spread evenly. Bake in 350°F (175°C) oven for 15 to 20 minutes until wooden pick inserted in centre comes out clean. Let stand in pan on wire rack for 5 minutes. Run knife around inside edges of pan to loosen cake.

Spread large tea towel on work surface. Cover with sheet of waxed paper. Sift second amount of cocoa onto waxed paper. Invert cake onto cocoa. Carefully peel off and discard waxed paper from bottom of cake. Roll up cake from short end, using towel and waxed paper as a guide. Let stand until cool.

Filling: Beat first 4 ingredients in small bowl until thick. Unroll cake. Spread half of filling evenly over cake, leaving 1/2 inch (12 mm) border. Roll up gently, discarding waxed paper. Place roll, seam-side down, on serving plate. Chill until firm.

(continued on next page)

Place marshmallow on roll to form a "knot." Spread remaining filling on roll and marshmallow. Place pecan halves randomly on roll. Cuts into 12 slices.

1 slice: 303 Calories; 17.6 g Total Fat (5.6 g Mono, 1.0 g Poly, 10.1 g Sat); 153 mg Cholesterol; 33 g Carbohydrate; 2 g Fibre; 5 g Protein; 49 mg Sodium

Pictured below.

A tiny touch of sherry will help you all make merry! Be sure to use a clear dish or a trifle bowl so all your guests can feast their eyes on the decadent layers before feasting their taste buds on this confection of cake, cream and custard.

Sherry Trifle

Box of white cake mix (2 layer size)	1	1
Raspberry jam	1 cup	250 mL
Milk	2 2/3 cups	650 mL
Custard powder	1/4 cup	60 mL
Granulated sugar	1/4 cup	60 mL
Milk	1/3 cup	75 mL
Vanilla extract	3/4 tsp.	4 mL
Medium sherry	1/3 cup	75 mL
Reserved raspberry syrup		
Container of frozen raspberries in syrup, thawed, drained and syrup reserved	15 oz.	425 g
TOPPING		
Whipping cream	1 cup	250 mL
Granulated sugar	1 tbsp.	15 mL
Vanilla extract	1/2 tsp.	2 mL

Prepare cake mix according to package directions, using two 8 inch (20 cm) round cake pans. Let stand in pans on wire rack until cooled completely. Remove from pans. Cut cakes in half horizontally to make thin layers.

Spread 1/4 cup (60 mL) jam on each layer. Cut into cubes. Set aside.

Heat first amount of milk in medium heavy saucepan on medium until hot, but not boiling.

Combine custard powder and sugar in small bowl. Add second amount of milk and vanilla. Stir. Slowly add to hot milk, stirring constantly with whisk, until boiling and thickened. Cool completely. Set aside.

Combine sherry and reserved raspberry syrup in separate small bowl.

To assemble, layer ingredients in 2 quart (2 L) glass bowl as follows:

1. Half of cake cubes
2. Half of sherry mixture
3. Half of raspberries
4. Half of custard

(continued on next page)

5. Remaining cake cubes
6. Remaining sherry mixture
7. Remaining raspberries
8. Remaining custard

Chill, covered, until cold.

Topping: Beat first 3 ingredients in small bowl until soft peaks form. Spread evenly over top layer of custard. Serves 12.

1 serving: 525 Calories; 17.0 g Total Fat (6.3 g Mono, 2.6 g Poly, 7.2 g Sat); 43 mg Cholesterol; 87 g Carbohydrate; 2 g Fibre; 7 g Protein; 314 mg Sodium

Pictured below.

Enjoy all the holiday flavours of eggnog in a rich and creamy cheesecake.

christmas fun

France, Britain and the United States have long battled over who is the true originator of eggnog, the all-time favourite Christmas beverage. Most food historians agree that the original, non-alcoholic version was probably French in origin. The oddly named *lait de poule* (chicken's milk!) was doctored with rum at some point—but who is responsible? That answer still remains highly debatable— perhaps you can ponder it while you sip your nog?

Eggnog Cheesecake

VANILLA WAFER CRUST

Coarsely crushed vanilla wafers (about 40)	1 1/2 cups	375 mL
Butter (or hard margarine)	1/3 cup	75 mL
Granulated sugar	1 tbsp.	15 mL

FILLING

Blocks of cream cheese (8 oz., 250 g, each), softened	3	3
Granulated sugar	2/3 cup	150 mL
Rum extract	2 1/2 tsp.	12 mL
Vanilla extract	1 tsp.	5 mL
Ground nutmeg	1/2 tsp.	2 mL
Large eggs	3	3
Sour cream	1 cup	250 mL

SAUCE

Water	1 cup	250 mL
Brown sugar, packed	2/3 cup	150 mL
Butter (or hard margarine)	1 tbsp.	15 mL
Salt	1/4 tsp.	1 mL
Water	1/4 cup	60 mL
Cornstarch	4 tsp.	20 mL
Rum extract	1/2 tsp.	2 mL
Vanilla extract	1/2 tsp.	2 mL

Vanilla Wafer Crust: Process crushed wafers in blender or food processor until fine crumbs form. Melt butter in medium saucepan on medium. Remove from heat. Add wafer crumbs and sugar. Mix well. Press firmly in greased 9 inch (22 cm) springform pan. Bake in 350°F (175°C) oven for about 10 minutes until browned and firm. Let stand in pan on wire rack until cool.

Filling: Beat cream cheese and sugar in large bowl until smooth. Add next 3 ingredients. Beat well.

Add eggs, 1 at a time, beating well after each addition. Add sour cream. Beat well. Spread evenly over crust. Bake in 325°F (160°C) oven for 55 to 60 minutes until centre is almost set. Run knife around inside edge of pan to allow cheesecake to settle evenly. Let stand in pan on wire rack until cooled completely. Chill, covered, for at least 6 hours or overnight.

(continued on next page)

Sauce: Combine first 4 ingredients in medium saucepan. Bring to a boil on medium.

Stir second amount of water into cornstarch in small cup. Add to brown sugar mixture. Heat and stir until thickened. Remove from heat.

Add rum and vanilla extracts. Stir well. Cool. Drizzle over individual servings of cheesecake. Cuts into 12 wedges.

1 wedge with 2 tbsp. (30 mL) sauce: 479 Calories; 34.3 g Total Fat (9.3 g Mono, 1.1 g Poly, 20.5 g Sat); 148 mg Cholesterol; 37 g Carbohydrate; trace Fiber; 7 g Protein; 346 mg Sodium

Pictured below.

This recipe makes enough mincemeat for four pies or plenty of tarts. Freeze for up to three months.

about suet

You've probably seen seed-covered suet in the grocery store, but stay away from that—it's truly for the birds. Proper cooking suet is harder fat from either a sheep or cow that can be easily obtained from a butcher—no birdseed included! It is great for many cooking applications, especially for baking, because it has a very high melting point and allows puddings and pastries to hold their shape until they begin to harden. If the thought of suet takes away your appetite, try substituting solid vegetable shortening.

Making the Mincemeat, above, is the hard part, putting the pies together is a snap—and they're sure to bring a touch of nostalgia to your holiday table.

Mincemeat

Chopped peeled cooking apple (such as McIntosh)	6 cups	1.5 L
Brown sugar, packed	4 cups	1 L
Chopped citron peel	2 cups	500 mL
Currants	2 cups	500 mL
Dark raisins	2 cups	500 mL
Apple juice	1 cup	250 mL
Granulated sugar	1 cup	250 mL
Ground beef suet	1 cup	250 mL
Lemon juice	1 cup	250 mL
Grated lemon zest (see Tip, page 23)	3 tbsp.	50 mL
Ground cinnamon	4 tsp.	20 mL
Ground allspice	2 tsp.	10 mL
Ground nutmeg	1 tsp.	5 mL
Ground cloves	1/2 tsp.	2 mL
Brandy (or rum) extract (optional)	1 tbsp.	15 mL

Combine first 14 ingredients in large saucepan. Heat and stir on medium until boiling. Reduce heat to medium-low. Simmer, uncovered, for 30 minutes, stirring often.

Add extract. Stir. Cool completely. Store in airtight containers in freezer for up to 6 months. Makes about 8 cups (2 L).

2 tbsp. (30 mL): 118 Calories; 3.3 g Total Fat (1.1 g Mono, 0.1 g Poly, 1.8 g Sat); 2 mg Cholesterol; 23 g Carbohydrate; 1 g Fibre; trace Protein; 7 mg Sodium

Mincemeat Pie

Mincemeat, above	2 cups	500 mL
Unsweetened applesauce	3/4 cup	175 mL
Minute tapioca	1 1/2 tbsp.	25 mL
Pastry for 2 crust 9 inch (22 cm) pie Water		
Granulated sugar	1/4 tsp.	1 mL

(continued on next page)

Combine first 3 ingredients in small bowl.

Divide pastry into 2 portions, making 1 portion slightly larger than the other. Shape each portion into slightly flattened disc. Roll out larger portion on lightly floured surface to about 1/8 inch (3 mm) thickness. Line 9 inch (22 cm) pie plate. Pour mincemeat mixture into shell. Spread evenly. Roll out smaller portion on lightly floured surface to about 1/8 inch (3 cm) thickness. Dampen edge of shell with water. Cover mincemeat mixture with pastry. Trim and crimp decorative edge to seal. Cut several small vents in top to allow steam to escape.

Sprinkle sugar over top. Bake on bottom rack in 400°F (205°C) oven for 30 to 35 minutes until golden. Let stand on wire rack until cooled completely. Cuts into 8 wedges.

1 wedge: 274 Calories; 10.8 g Total Fat (1.3 g Mono, 0.2 g Poly, 5.1 g Sat); 8 mg Cholesterol; 44 g Carbohydrate; 1 g Fibre; 1 g Protein; 109 mg Sodium

Pictured below.

Mincemeat Pie, page 94

mincemeat tarts

Rather have single-sized servings on hand? Spoon your mincemeat mixture into 36 unbaked tart shells. Bake in 400°F (205°C) oven for about 20 minutes until the pastry is golden.

Cranberries change traditional apple pie into a Christmas favourite. Delicious with vanilla or eggnog-flavoured ice cream.

Bake these scrumptious pies up to 24 hours ahead of time and store at room temperature until ready to serve.

Christmas Cranapple Pies

Brown sugar, packed	1 1/2 cups	375 mL
All-purpose flour	1/4 cup	60 mL
Ground allspice	1/2 tsp.	2 mL
Ground cinnamon	1/2 tsp.	2 mL
Ground nutmeg	1/4 tsp.	1 mL
Sliced peeled tart apple (such as Granny Smith)	8 cups	2 L
Lemon juice	1 tbsp.	15 mL
Vanilla extract	1 tsp.	5 mL
Dried cranberries	2 cups	500 mL
Pastry for 2 double crust 9 inch (22 cm) pies		
Water		
Large egg, fork-beaten	1	1
Granulated sugar	2 tsp.	10 mL

Combine first 5 ingredients in small bowl.

Put next 3 ingredients into large bowl. Toss until coated. Add cranberries and brown sugar mixture. Toss until coated.

Divide pastry into 4 portions, making 2 portions slightly larger than the others. Shape each portion into slightly flattened disc. Roll out 2 larger portions, 1 at a time, on lightly floured surface to about 1/8 inch (3 mm) thickness. Line two 9 inch (22 cm) pie plates. Spoon fruit mixture into shells. Roll out remaining 2 pastry portions, 1 at a time, on lightly floured surface to about 1/8 inch (3 mm) thickness. Dampen edges of shells with water. Cover fruit mixture with pastry. Trim and crimp decorative edges to seal.

Brush tops of pies with egg. Sprinkle with granulated sugar. Cut several small vents in tops to allow steam to escape. Bake on bottom rack in 375°F (190°C) oven for about 1 hour until golden and apple is tender. Let stand on wire racks until cooled completely. Each pie cuts into 8 wedges, for a total of 16 wedges.

1 wedge: 307 Calories; 7.3 g Total Fat (0 g Mono, 0 g Poly, 3.1 g Sat); 18 mg Cholesterol; 62 g Carbohydrate; 3 g Fibre; 2 g Protein; 114 mg Sodium

Pictured at right.

Everyone will adore these cute little pumpkin pies. They go perfectly with Maple Orange Whipped Cream, below.

Mini Pumpkin Pies

Pastry for 2 crust 9 inch (22 cm) pie

Large eggs	2	2
Can of pure pumpkin (no spices)	14 oz.	398 mL
Can of evaporated milk	13 1/2 oz.	385 mL
Granulated sugar	1/2 cup	125 mL
Brown sugar, packed	1/4 cup	60 mL
Ground cinnamon	1 tsp.	5 mL
Ground ginger	1/2 tsp.	2 mL
Ground cloves	1/4 tsp.	1 mL

Roll out pastry on lightly floured surface to about 1/8 inch (3 mm) thickness. Cut into sixteen 4 inch (10 cm) circles. Press circles into bottom and sides of 16 ungreased muffin cups. Cover with plastic wrap. Chill for 30 minutes.

Whisk eggs in large bowl for about 2 minutes until frothy.

Add remaining 7 ingredients. Beat until smooth. Pour pumpkin mixture into shells. Bake on bottom rack in 375°F (190°C) oven for about 40 minutes until wooden pick inserted in centre of pie comes out clean. Let stand in pan until cool. Remove pies from pan and place on wire rack to cool completely. Makes 16 mini-pies.

1 mini-pie: 199 Calories; 8.2 g Total Fat (0.2 g Mono, trace Poly, 3.6 g Sat); 34 mg Cholesterol; 28 g Carbohydrate; 1 g Fibre; 4 g Protein; 141 mg Sodium

Pictured at right.

The flavours of maple and orange liqueur make the ordinary extraordinary in this fantastic dessert topping. Sure to win rave reviews from your dinner guests, try with Mini Pumpkin Pies, above, cake, apple crisp or even coffee!

Maple Orange Whipped Cream

Whipping cream	2 cups	500 mL
Maple (or maple-flavoured) syrup	1/4 cup	60 mL
Orange liqueur	3 tbsp.	50 mL

Beat all 3 ingredients in large bowl on medium-high until soft peaks form. Makes about 4 cups (1 L).

1/4 cup (60 mL): 121 Calories; 10.4 g Total Fat (3.0 g Mono, 0.4 g Poly, 6.5 g Sat); 38 mg Cholesterol; 6 g Carbohydrate; 0 g Fibre; 1 g Protein; 11 mg Sodium

Pictured at right.

Butter Tarts

Unbaked tart shells	12	12
Dark raisins (or currants), coarsely chopped	1/3 cup	75 mL
Butter (or hard margarine), softened	3 tbsp.	50 mL
Brown sugar, packed	1/2 cup	125 mL
Large egg, fork-beaten	1	1
Golden corn syrup	1/4 cup	60 mL
White vinegar	1 1/2 tsp.	7 mL
Vanilla extract	1/4 tsp.	1 mL
Salt	1/8 tsp.	0.5 mL

Stock up your freezer with these delicious butter tarts for a convenient treat to serve when guests drop by during the holiday season. Use store-bought tart shells for easy preparation.

Arrange tart shells on baking sheet with sides. Sprinkle raisins into shells.

Beat butter and brown sugar in small bowl until smooth. Add remaining 5 ingredients. Mix well. Spoon over raisins. Tart shells should be about 2/3 full. Bake on bottom rack in 375°F (190°C) oven for about 15 minutes until pastry is golden and filling is domed. Cool. Makes 12 tarts.

1 tart: 185 Calories; 8.8 g Total Fat (3.1 g Mono, 2.2 g Poly, 2.8 g Sat); 25 mg Cholesterol; 26 g Carbohydrate; trace Fibre; 1 g Protein; 174 mg Sodium

Left: Maple Orange Whipped Cream, page 98
Right: Mini Pumpkin Pies, page 98

The perfect chocolatey square to put out for guests. We've added a festively-coloured cherry filling instead of the classic custard centre.

peppermint nanaimo bars

Add a little green to your dessert tray by making a peppermint middle layer instead of a cherry one. Just increase the butter (or hard margarine) to 1/3 cup (75 mL) and use the same amount of icing (confectioner's) sugar. Add in 3 tbsp. (50 mL) milk and 1 tsp. (5 mL) peppermint extract. Beat until smooth, adding more icing sugar or milk until spreading consistency. Add enough green food colouring until pale green.

Pictured at right.

Chocolate Cherry Nanaimo Bars

BOTTOM LAYER

Butter (or hard margarine), softened	1/2 cup	125 mL
Cocoa, sifted if lumpy	1/3 cup	75 mL
Granulated sugar	1/4 cup	60 mL
Large egg, fork-beaten	1	1
Graham cracker crumbs	1 3/4 cups	425 mL
Fine (or medium) unsweetened coconut	3/4 cup	175 mL
Finely chopped walnuts	1/2 cup	125 mL

MIDDLE LAYER

Butter (or hard margarine), softened	1/4 cup	60 mL
Icing (confectioner's) sugar	2 cups	500 mL
Maraschino cherry juice	2 tbsp.	30 mL
Almond extract	1 tsp.	5 mL
Chopped maraschino cherries, drained and blotted dry	1/3 cup	75 mL

TOP LAYER

Semi-sweet chocolate chips (see Note)	2/3 cup	150 mL
Butter (or hard margarine)	2 tbsp.	30 mL

Bottom Layer: Heat and stir first 3 ingredients in medium heavy saucepan on medium until butter is melted.

Add egg. Heat and stir until thickened. Remove from heat.

Add next 3 ingredients. Stir. Press firmly in ungreased 9 x 9 inch (22 x 22 cm) pan.

Middle Layer: Beat first 4 ingredients in medium bowl on low until combined. Beat on high until light.

Add cherries. Stir. Spread evenly over bottom layer. Let stand for 10 minutes. Pat smooth.

Top Layer: Heat chocolate chips and butter in small heavy saucepan on lowest heat, stirring often, until chocolate chips are almost melted. Do not overheat. Remove from heat. Stir until smooth. Cool slightly. Spread evenly over middle layer. Chill until set. Cuts into 36 squares.

(continued on next page)

1 square: 130 Calories; 8.1 g Total Fat (1.9 g Mono, 1.2 g Poly, 4.5 g Sat); 17 mg Cholesterol;
15 g Carbohydrate; 1 g Fibre; 1 g Protein; 59 mg Sodium

Pictured below.

Note: You can use four 1 oz. (28 g) semi-sweet chocolate baking squares instead
of the chocolate chips.

Bottom left: Chocolate Cherry Nanaimo Bars, page 100
Bottom right: Peppermint Nanaimo Bars, page 100

These sweet and colourful bars make a splendid holiday treat. Although not technically marzipan, the taste and texture are similar but the effort required is considerably less!

Marzipan Bars

BOTTOM LAYER

Pastry for 9 inch (22 cm) pie shell		
Raspberry jam	1/4 cup	60 mL

MIDDLE LAYER

Butter (or hard margarine), softened	1/2 cup	125 mL
Granulated sugar	2/3 cup	150 mL
Large eggs	2	2
Rice flour	2/3 cup	150 mL
Salt	1/4 tsp.	1 mL
Drop of red liquid food coloring	1	1
Drop of green liquid food coloring	1	1

ALMOND ICING

Icing (confectioner's) sugar	1 1/2 cups	375 mL
Butter (or hard margarine), softened	3 tbsp.	50 mL
Milk	1 1/2 tbsp.	25 mL
Almond extract	1 tsp.	5 mL

Bottom Layer: Press pastry into bottom of ungreased 9 x 9 inch (22 x 22 cm) pan. Spread jam over pastry.

Middle Layer: Cream butter and sugar in medium bowl. Add eggs, 1 at a time, beating well after each addition until fluffy.

Stir in rice flour and salt. Divide batter into 2 equal portions. Add red food colouring to 1 portion. Mix well. Add green food colouring to remaining portion. Mix well. Drop by rounded teaspoonfuls, alternating colours, over jam to make a checkerboard pattern. It will spread flat as it bakes. Bake on bottom rack in 375°F (190°C) oven for about 25 minutes until golden. Cool.

Almond Icing: Beat all 4 ingredients in small bowl until smooth. Spread evenly over middle layer. Cuts into 36 squares.

1 square: 111 Calories; 5.3 g Total Fat (0.9 g Mono, 0.1 g Poly, 3.0 g Sat); 22 mg Cholesterol; 15 g Carbohydrate; trace Fibre; 1 g Protein; 67 mg Sodium

Pictured on page 105.

Caramel Slice

Butter (or hard margarine)	1/4 cup	60 mL
Brown sugar, packed	1 cup	250 mL
Large egg, fork-beaten	1	1
Medium unsweetened coconut	1 cup	250 mL
All-purpose flour	3/4 cup	175 mL
Chopped walnuts	1/2 cup	125 mL
Baking powder	1 tsp.	5 mL
Salt	1/4 tsp.	1 mL
CARAMEL ICING		
Brown sugar, packed	1/2 cup	125 mL
Butter (or hard margarine)	1/4 cup	60 mL
Milk	2 tbsp.	30 mL
Icing (confectioner's) sugar	1 cup	250 mL

Melt butter in large saucepan on medium. Remove from heat. Add brown sugar. Stir. Add egg. Stir.

Add next 5 ingredients. Stir well. Spread evenly in greased 9 x 9 inch (22 x 22 cm) pan. Bake in 350°F (175°C) oven for about 30 minutes until set and edges start to turn golden.

Caramel Icing: Heat and stir first 3 ingredients in small saucepan on medium until melted. Bring to a boil. Reduce heat to medium-low. Simmer, uncovered, for 2 minutes, stirring occasionally. Cool.

Add icing sugar. Stir until light and creamy, adding more icing sugar or milk if necessary until spreading consistency. Spread evenly over top. Let stand until icing is firm. Cuts into 36 squares.

1 square: 105 Calories; 5.1 g Total Fat (0.9 g Mono, 0.9 g Poly, 2.9 g Sat); 13 mg Cholesterol; 15 g Carbohydrate; trace Fibre; 1 g Protein; 48 mg Sodium

Pictured on page 105.

You have eggnog lovers, you have chocolate lovers and then you have caramel lovers! These walnut-laden squares are sure to impress anyone with a caramel craving.

time-saving tip

To cool the caramel icing quickly, set the saucepan in cold water in a large bowl or in the sink. Do not let the water get into the saucepan. Stir until cooled.

Having trouble deciding what to bake for Christmas this year? Why not make one delicious square that combines several delicious flavours? Shortbread, chocolate and orange go so well together!

christmas fun

Charles Dickens' *A Christmas Carol*, written in 1843, has been performed and filmed more than any other Christmas tale. The story perfectly details the redemption of a man stingy in heart and soul who learns the error of his ways when he is visited by three Christmas Spirits. More than any other narrative, *A Christmas Carol* depicts Christmas as being that special time of year when miracles do happen.

Orange Chocolate Squares

BOTTOM LAYER		
All-purpose flour	2 cups	500 mL
Butter (or hard margarine), softened	1 cup	250 mL
Brown sugar, packed	1/2 cup	125 mL
MIDDLE LAYER		
Large eggs	4	4
Granulated sugar	1 cup	250 mL
Orange juice	1/3 cup	75 mL
All-purpose flour	1/4 cup	60 mL
Grated orange zest (see Tip, page 23)	1 tbsp.	15 mL
Baking powder	1 tsp.	5 mL
TOPPING		
Semi-sweet chocolate chips	1/2 cup	125 mL

Bottom Layer: Mix first 3 ingredients in large bowl until mixture resembles coarse crumbs. Press firmly in ungreased 9 x 13 inch (22 x 33 cm) pan. Bake in 350°F (175°C) oven for about 15 minutes until golden.

Middle Layer: Beat eggs in medium bowl until frothy. Add next 5 ingredients. Mix well. Pour over bottom layer. Bake in 325°F (160°C) oven for about 25 minutes until firm.

Topping: Heat chocolate chips in small heavy saucepan on lowest heat, stirring often, until almost melted. Do not overheat. Remove from heat. Stir until smooth. Drizzle over middle layer. Let stand until cool. Cuts into 54 squares.

1 square: 81 Calories; 4.2 g Total Fat (1.0 g Mono, 0.1 g Poly, 2.5 g Sat); 25 mg Cholesterol; 10 g Carbohydrate; trace Fibre; 1 g Protein; 35 mg Sodium

Pictured at right.

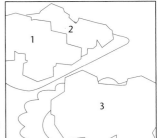

1. Caramel Slice, page 103
2. Orange Chocolate Squares, above
3. Marzipan Bars, page 102

This unique, quick and easy brittle cuts into attractive squares or can be broken into more eclectic shapes. It makes a great addition to anyone's snack tray.

christmas fun

The use of mistletoe during the Christmas season can be linked way back to the Druids and their mid-winter rites. It wasn't until much later that the notion of smooching under the mistletoe came into being. According to folklore: no woman standing under the mistletoe can refuse to be kissed; kissing can lead to marriage or a great friendship; and if the mistletoe isn't burned before the twelfth night, no one kissed under it will be married that year.

Breton Brittle

Dare Breton crackers (see Note)	28	28
Butter (or hard margarine)	1 cup	250 mL
Brown sugar, packed	1 cup	250 mL
TOPPING:		
Semi-sweet chocolate chips	1 2/3 cups	400 mL
Finely chopped pecans (or walnuts)	1/3 cup	75 mL

Arrange crackers in foil-lined 9 x 13 inch (22 x 33 cm) pan, overlapping 4 crackers crosswise and 7 crackers lengthwise, to cover bottom.

Combine butter and brown sugar in small saucepan. Heat and stir on medium until melted. Bring to a boil. Carefully pour over crackers. Bake in 400°F (205°C) oven for 5 minutes.

Topping: Sprinkle chocolate chips over top. Let stand until chips are softened. Spread evenly. Sprinkle with pecans. Let stand until cool. Cuts into 28 squares.

1 square: 167 Calories; 11.5 g Total Fat (3.3 g Mono, 0.6 g Poly, 6.6 g Sat); 17 mg Cholesterol; 17 g Carbohydrate; 1 g Fibre; 1 g Protein; 93 mg Sodium

Note: If Dare Breton crackers are not available in your area, use another type of thin, round 2 1/2 inch (6.4 cm) crackers (not soda) to line your pan.

Almond Fruit Bark

Dark (or white) chocolate bars (3 1/2 oz., 100 g, each), chopped	4	4
Dried cherries	1/2 cup	125 mL
Whole natural almonds, toasted (see Tip, page 72)	1/2 cup	125 mL
Chopped dried apricot	1/3 cup	75 mL

A tempting fruit-and-nut chocolate treat. Package in beribboned plastic bags for gift giving.

Heat chocolate in medium heavy saucepan on lowest heat, stirring often, until almost melted. Do not overheat. Remove from heat. Stir until smooth.

Add remaining 3 ingredients. Mix well. Spread evenly on waxed paper-lined baking sheet with sides. Chill for about 30 minutes until set. Remove from pan. Break into irregular-shaped pieces, about 1 1/2 × 4 inches (3.8 × 10 cm) each. Store in airtight container in freezer for up to 1 month. Makes about 24 pieces.

1 piece: 122 Calories; 6.0 g Total Fat (0.9 g Mono, 0.3 g Poly, 3.6 g Sat); 1 mg Cholesterol; 14 g Carbohydrate; 2 g Fibre; 2 g Protein; 1 mg Sodium

Pictured below.

Forget fudge that takes all day to make. Our five-minute miracle fudge can compare with any of those more fussy recipes.

Five-Minute Fudge

Granulated sugar	1 2/3 cups	400 mL
Evaporated milk (or half-and-half cream)	2/3 cup	150 mL
Butter (or hard margarine)	2 tbsp.	30 mL
Salt	1/2 tsp.	2 mL
Miniature marshmallows	2 cups	500 mL
Semi-sweet chocolate chips	1 1/2 cups	375 mL
Chopped walnuts	1/2 cup	125 mL
Vanilla extract	1 tsp.	5 mL

Combine first 4 ingredients in medium heavy saucepan. Bring to a boil on medium. Boil gently for 5 minutes, stirring constantly. Remove from heat.

Add remaining 4 ingredients. Stir. Beat with spoon for about 1 minute until marshmallows are melted. Spread evenly in greased 8 × 8 inch (20 × 20 cm) pan. Let stand until set. Makes about 2 lbs. (900 g) fudge. Cuts into 36 squares.

1 square: 100 Calories; 3.9 g Total Fat (1.0 g Mono, 0.9 g Poly, 1.8 g Sat); 2 mg Cholesterol; 17 g Carbohydrate; 1 g Fibre; 1 g Protein; 47 mg Sodium

Pictured on page 111 and on back cover.

Find pure bliss by letting a piece of Old-Fashioned Toffee melt in your mouth. The rich, sweet flavour can't be beat.

Old-Fashioned Toffee

Brown sugar, packed	1 1/4 cups	300 mL
Can of sweetened condensed milk	11 oz.	300 mL
Butter	1/4 cup	60 mL
Corn syrup	1/4 cup	60 mL

Combine all 4 ingredients in medium heavy saucepan. Bring to a boil on medium-low, stirring constantly. Heat and stir until firm ball stage (242° to 248°F, 117° to 120°C) on candy thermometer (see Tip, page 24) or until small amount dropped into very cold water forms a pliable ball. Spread evenly in well greased 8 × 8 inch (20 × 20 cm) pan. Let stand for 10 minutes. Score top of toffee into 1 inch (2.5 cm) squares using sharp knife. Cool completely. Remove from pan. Break into squares. Makes 64 squares.

1 square: 47 Calories; 1.3 g Total Fat (0.3 g Mono, 0.1 g Poly, 0.8 g Sat); 4 mg Cholesterol; 9 g Carbohydrate; 0 g Fibre; 1 g Protein; 17 mg Sodium

Pictured on page 111 and on back cover.

Orange Cookies

Butter (or hard margarine), softened	1/2 cup	125 mL
Granulated sugar	1 cup	250 mL
Large egg	1	1
Plain yogurt	1/2 cup	125 mL
Orange juice	1 tbsp.	15 mL
Vanilla extract	1/4 tsp.	1 mL
All-purpose flour	2 cups	500 mL
Ground almonds	1/4 cup	60 mL
Grated orange zest (see Tip, page 23)	1 tbsp.	15 mL
Baking powder	2 tsp.	10 mL
Baking soda	1/2 tsp.	2 mL
Salt	1/2 tsp.	2 mL

Cream butter and sugar in large bowl. Add next 4 ingredients. Beat well.

Combine remaining 6 ingredients in medium bowl. Add to butter mixture in 2 additions, mixing well after each addition until no dry flour remains. Drop, using 1 1/2 tbsp. (25 mL) for each cookie, about 1 inch (2.5 cm) apart onto greased cookie sheets. Bake in 375°F (190°C) oven for about 10 minutes until lightly golden. Let stand on cookie sheets for 5 minutes. Remove cookies from cookie sheet and place on wire racks to cool. Makes about 48 cookies.

1 cookie: 57 Calories; 2.4 g Total Fat (0.7 g Mono, 0.1 g Poly, 1.4 g Sat); 10 mg Cholesterol; 8 g Carbohydrate; trace Fibre; 1 g Protein; 65 mg Sodium

Pictured on page 115.

These tasty little drop cookies have just the right amount of orange flavour. Orange you glad you baked them?

about stand time

Though it's so tempting to pop a warm cookie straight into your mouth, standing time is very important. Not only does it keep you from scalding your tongue on too-hot goodies, it allows baked goods time to cool and retain their shape.

Peanut butter makes these decadent chocolate-coated cherries unique.

Chocolate Cherries

Cocktail cherries with stems, drained and blotted dry	40	40
Icing (confectioner's) sugar	2 cups	500 mL
Smooth peanut butter	1 cup	250 mL
Butter (or hard margarine), softened	2 tbsp.	30 mL
Dark chocolate melting wafers	1 3/4 cups	425 mL

Arrange cherries on paper towel-lined plate. Let stand at room temperature for at least 6 hours or overnight until dry.

Combine next 3 ingredients in medium bowl. Divide into 40 equal portions. Mold peanut butter mixture around cherries, covering completely.

Heat chocolate wafers in small heavy saucepan on lowest heat, stirring constantly, until almost melted. Do not overheat. Remove from heat. Stir until smooth. Let stand for 5 minutes. Dip cherries into chocolate. Place on waxed paper-lined baking sheet with sides. Let stand until set. Store in airtight container in refrigerator for up to 2 months. Makes 40 cherries.

1 cherry: 123 Calories; 7.0 g Total Fat (0.2 g Mono, trace Poly, 2.7 g Sat); 1.5 mg Cholesterol; 16 g Carbohydrate; 1 g Fibre; 2 g Protein; 37 mg Sodium

Pictured at right and on back cover.

These sweet pecan treats literally melt in your mouth—and they're so easy to make!

Pecan Balls

All-purpose flour	2 1/4 cups	550 mL
Butter (or hard margarine), softened	1 cup	250 mL
Ground pecans	1 cup	250 mL
Icing (confectioner's) sugar	1/2 cup	125 mL
Vanilla extract	2 tsp.	10 mL
Icing (confectioner's) sugar	1/2 cup	125 mL

Put first 5 ingredients into large bowl. Mix until no dry flour remains. Roll into 1 inch (2.5 cm) balls. Arrange about 1 inch (2.5 cm) apart on ungreased baking sheet with sides. Bake in 325°F (160°C) oven for 20 to 25 minutes until golden. Let stand on baking sheet for 5 minutes.

(continued on next page)

Roll balls in icing sugar until coated. Makes about 72 balls.

1 ball: 53 Calories; 3.7 g Total Fat (1.3 g Mono, 0.5 g Poly, 1.7 g Sat); 7 mg Cholesterol; 5 g Carbohydrate; trace Fibre; 1 g Protein; 18 mg Sodium

Pictured below and on back cover.

buried cherry balls

Completely bury one maraschino cherry, drained and blotted dry, in each dough ball. Bake as directed and when sufficiently cooled, roll in icing sugar.

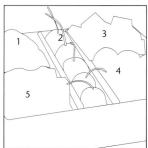

These tasty rum balls can be made in mere minutes. For variety, try rolling them in chocolate sprinkles or cocoa instead of icing sugar.

Rum Balls

Vanilla wafer crumbs	3 cups	750 mL
Icing (confectioner's) sugar	1 cup	250 mL
Ground almonds (or pecans)	1/2 cup	125 mL
Water	1/3 cup	75 mL
Cocoa, sifted if lumpy	3 tbsp.	50 mL
Corn syrup	3 tbsp.	50 mL
Rum extract	2 tsp.	10 mL
Icing (confectioner's) sugar	2 tbsp.	30 mL

Combine first 7 ingredients in medium bowl. Roll into 1 inch (2.5 cm) balls.

Roll each ball in second amount of icing sugar until coated. Let stand in airtight container at room temperature for at least 2 days before serving. Makes about 36 balls.

1 ball: 119 Calories; 4.4 g Total Fat (2.6 g Mono, 0.6 g Poly, 1.0 g Sat); 0 mg Cholesterol; 19 g Carbohydrate; 1 g Fibre; 1 g Protein; 61 mg Sodium

Pictured on page 111 and on back cover.

Store-bought truffles? No thanks! Your guests will be very impressed when you tell them you made these decadent darlings yourself!

about clear vanilla

Clear vanilla is usually a double-strength imitation vanilla. Natural vanilla is brown and can make white icing quite drab looking, whereas clear vanilla keeps white its whitest! You can find clear vanilla at kitchen specialty stores.

White Chocolate Fudge Truffles

Granulated sugar	1 1/2 cups	375 mL
Evaporated milk (or half-and-half cream)	1/2 cup	125 mL
White chocolate chips	1 cup	250 mL
Butter, softened	1/3 cup	75 mL
Clear vanilla	2 tsp.	10 mL
Salt, just a pinch		
Dark (or milk) chocolate melting wafers	1/2 cup	125 mL
Pink candy melting wafers	1/2 cup	125 mL
White candy melting wafers	1/2 cup	125 mL

Combine sugar and evaporated milk in large heavy saucepan. Heat and stir on medium for about 4 minutes until mixture comes to a rolling boil that cannot be stirred down. Reduce heat to medium-low to keep a hard boil without boiling over. Boil for 6 minutes, stirring occasionally. Remove from heat.

(continued on next page)

Combine next 4 ingredients in small bowl. Add to evaporated milk mixture. Beat with electric mixer in saucepan for about 8 minutes until soft peaks form. Pour into greased 8 × 8 inch (20 × 20 cm) pan. Chill until firm enough to roll into balls. Drop, using 1 1/2 tsp. (7 mL) for each truffle, onto cold waxed paper-lined baking sheet with sides. If mxture becomes too soft to work with, return to refrigerator. Roll into balls. Chill until firm.

Heat chocolate melting wafers in small heavy saucepan on lowest heat, stirring constantly, until almost melted. Do not overheat. Remove from heat. Stir until smooth. Place 1 ball on top of fork. Dip into chocolate until completely coated, allowing excess to drip back into saucepan. Place on same waxed paper-lined baking sheet. Repeat with 1/3 of balls. Repeat with pink melting wafers, white melting wafers and remaining balls. Drizzle any remaining melted chocolate in decorative pattern over balls. Chill until set. Makes about 48 truffles.

1 truffle: 68 Calories; 3.2 g Total Fat (0.9 g Mono, 0.1 g Poly, 1.9 g Sat); 4 mg Cholesterol; 10 g Carbohydrate; trace Fibre; 1 g Protein; 15 mg Sodium

Pictured below.

tip

To make truffles that are uniform in size, use a miniature ice cream scoop. If the truffles are not going to be dipped until the next day, place in an airtight container and chill to prevent drying.

White Chocolate Fudge Truffles, page 112

Put a zesty lemon twist on your regular shortbread.

storing shortbread

Shortbread cookies will keep for several weeks stored at room temperature in an airtight container. Or if having them sitting out on the counter is too much of a temptation, you can freeze them in an airtight container for up to six months.

Lemon Shortbread Slices

Butter (or hard margarine), softened	1 cup	250 mL
Granulated sugar	3/4 cup	175 mL
Grated lemon zest	2 tsp.	10 mL
All-purpose flour	2 1/4 cups	550 mL
Egg white (large), fork-beaten	1	1
Yellow sanding (decorating) sugar (see Note)	1/3 cup	75 mL

Cream butter and granulated sugar in large bowl. Add lemon zest. Beat well.

Add flour in 2 additions, mixing well after each addition until no dry flour remains. Roll into 3 inch (7.5 cm) diameter log.

Brush log with egg white.

Spread sanding sugar on sheet of waxed paper, slightly longer than log. Roll log in sanding sugar until coated. Wrap with plastic wrap. Chill for at least 6 hours or overnight. Discard plastic wrap. Cut into 1/4 inch (6 mm) slices. Cut each slice in half. Arrange about 1 inch (2.5 cm) apart on ungreased cookie sheets. Carefully score each half with knife from centre point of flat edge toward rounded edge to make 4 wedges on each (see diagram). Bake in 325°F (160°C) oven for 8 to 10 minutes until golden. Let stand on cookie sheets for 5 minutes. Remove cookies from cookie sheets and place on wire racks to cool. Makes about 78 cookies.

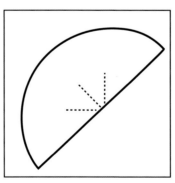

1 cookie: 42 Calories; 2.3 g Total Fat (0.6 g Mono, 0.1 g Poly, 1.5 g Sat); 6 mg Cholesterol; 5 g Carbohydrate; trace Fibre; trace Protein; 17 mg Sodium

Pictured on page 115.

Note: Sanding sugar is a coarse decorating sugar that comes in white and various colours and is available at specialty kitchen stores.

Snowballs

Butter (or hard margarine)	2 tbsp.	30 mL
Chopped pitted dates	3 cups	750 mL
Brown sugar, packed	1 cup	250 mL
Large eggs, fork-beaten	2	2
Crisp rice cereal	2 cups	500 mL
Chopped walnuts	1 cup	250 mL
Shredded coconut, approximately	1 cup	250 mL

Warning: a snowball fight may be looming—no one's going to give up the last of these coconut treats willingly!

Combine first 4 ingredients in large frying pan. Heat and stir on medium until mixture is melted and combined. Remove from heat.

Add cereal and walnuts. Mix well. Let stand for 10 minutes.

Spread coconut on large plate. Drop date mixture, using 1 tbsp. (15 mL) for each ball, onto coconut. Roll until coated. Roll between hands to make balls. Place balls on waxed paper-lined baking sheet with sides. Chill until firm. Makes about 48 balls.

1 ball: 81 Calories; 2.8 g Total Fat (0.4 g Mono, 1.2 g Poly, 1.0 g Sat); 10 mg Cholesterol; 14 g Carbohydrate; 1 g Fibre; 1 g Protein; 24 mg Sodium

Pictured below.

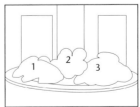

1. Lemon Shortbread Squares, page 114
2. Snowballs, above
3. Orange Cookies, page 109

What would the holidays be without gingerbread? Buy a few tubes of coloured cake decorating gel, and let the kids go crazy decorating the cookies.

about raw eggs

The icing for these cookies uses raw eggs. Make sure to use fresh, clean Grade A eggs with no cracks. Keep chilled and consume the same day it is prepared. Always discard leftovers. Pregnant women, young children or the elderly are not advised to eat anything containing raw egg.

Gingerbread Cookies

Butter (or hard margarine), softened	1/2 cup	125 mL
Granulated sugar	1/2 cup	125 mL
Fancy molasses	1/2 cup	125 mL
Egg yolk (large)	1	1
All-purpose flour	2 cups	500 mL
Baking powder	1/2 tsp.	2 mL
Baking soda	1/2 tsp.	2 mL
Ground cinnamon	1 tsp.	5 mL
Ground ginger	1 tsp.	5 mL
Ground cloves	1/2 tsp.	2 mL
Ground nutmeg	1/4 tsp.	1 mL
Salt	1/4 tsp.	1 mL
ICING		
Egg white (large)	1	1
Icing (confectioner's) sugar	2 cups	500 mL

Cream butter and sugar in large bowl. Add molasses and egg yolk. Beat until smooth.

Combine next 8 ingredients in small bowl. Add to butter mixture in 3 additions, mixing well after each addition. Wrap with plastic wrap. Chill for at least 1 hour. Roll out dough on lightly floured surface to 1/4 inch (6 mm) thickness. Cut out shapes with lightly floured cookie cutters. Roll out scraps to cut more shapes. Arrange about 1 inch (2.5 cm) apart on ungreased cookie sheet. Bake in 350°F (175°C) oven for 10 to 15 minutes until firm. Let stand on cookie sheet for 5 minutes. Remove cookies from cookie sheet and place on wire rack to cool.

Icing: Beat egg white with fork in medium bowl. Add icing sugar. Stir until smooth, adding more icing sugar if necessary until piping consistency. Spread or pipe over cookies. Makes 12 to 16 gingerbread men or a variety of other shaped cookies.

1 cookie: 287 Calories; 8.0 g Total Fat (2.1 g Mono, 0.4 g Poly, 5.0 g Sat); 37 mg Cholesterol; 52 g Carbohydrate; trace Fibre; 3 g Protein; 177 mg Sodium

Pictured at right.

A loaf with the traditional Christmas colours and an unusual, yet delicious, combination of flavours.

tip

Cutting gumdrops can be a gooey and sticky proposition. The mess will be minimal if you use greased kitchen shears or a very sharp greased knife.

Cranberry Mint Loaf

Fresh (or frozen, thawed) cranberries, coarsely chopped	1 cup	250 mL
Leaf-shaped spearmint gumdrops, diced (about 20)	1 cup	250 mL
All-purpose flour	1 tbsp.	15 mL
All-purpose flour	2 cups	500 mL
Baking powder	1 tsp.	5 mL
Baking soda	1/2 tsp.	2 mL
Salt	1/4 tsp.	1 mL
Butter (or hard margarine), softened	1/2 cup	125 mL
Granulated sugar	1 cup	250 mL
Large eggs	2	2
Milk	2/3 cup	150 mL
Grated lemon zest	2 tsp.	10 mL
Mint extract	1/2 tsp.	2 mL

Put first 3 ingredients into small bowl. Toss until coated. Set aside.

Combine next 4 ingredients in medium bowl.

Cream butter and sugar in large bowl. Add eggs, 1 at a time, beating well after each addition.

Add remaining 3 ingredients. Beat well. Add flour mixture and cranberry mixture. Stir until just moistened. Spread in greased 9 x 5 x 3 inch (22 x 12.5 x 7.5 cm) loaf pan. Bake in 350°F (175°C) oven for 60 to 65 minutes until wooden pick inserted in centre comes out clean. Let stand in pan for 10 minutes. Remove loaf from pan and place on wire rack to cool. Cuts into 18 slices.

1 slice: 187 Calories; 5.7 g Total Fat (1.3 g Mono, 0.2 g Poly, 3.5 g Sat); 38 mg Cholesterol; 32 g Carbohydrate; 1 g Fibre; 2 g Protein; 134 mg Sodium

Pictured on page 119.

Eggnog Candy Bread

All-purpose flour	2 1/4 cups	550 mL
Baking powder	2 tsp.	10 mL
Salt	1/2 tsp.	2 mL
Rolls of butterscotch-flavoured doughnut-shaped hard candies (3/4 oz., 25 g, each)	2	2
Large eggs	2	2
Eggnog	1 cup	250 mL
Granulated sugar	2/3 cup	150 mL
Cooking oil	1/3 cup	75 mL
Rum extract	2 tsp.	10 mL
Vanilla extract	1 tsp.	5 mL

If eggnog is one of your holiday favourites, you're sure to love this sweet, candy-filled loaf that combines the traditional flavours of rum and eggnog.

Measure first 3 ingredients into large bowl. Stir. Make a well in centre.

Put candies into medium resealable freezer bag. Seal bag. Pound with mallet or rolling pin until candies are broken into small pieces. Set aside 1 tbsp. (15 mL) in small cup. Sprinkle remaining candy pieces over flour mixture.

Beat remaining 6 ingredients in medium bowl. Add to well in flour mixture. Stir until just moistened. Spread in greased 9 × 5 × 3 inch (22 × 12.5 × 7.5 cm) loaf pan. Sprinkle reserved candy pieces over top. Bake in 350°F (175°C) oven for 50 to 55 minutes until wooden pick inserted in centre comes out clean. Let stand in pan for 10 minutes. Remove loaf from pan and place on wire rack to cool. Cuts into 18 slices.

1 slice: 154 Calories; 5.9 g Total Fat (2.7 g Mono, 1.2 g Poly, 1.3 g Sat); 33 mg Cholesterol; 23 g Carbohydrate; trace Fibre; 3 g Protein; 125 mg Sodium

Pictured below.

Left and right: Eggnog Candy Bread, above
Centre: Cranberry Mint Loaf, page 118

This fruitcake will make you sad Christmas comes but once a year. This recipe requires a little advance planning because it needs to be prepared at least three days before you want to serve it. Fruitcakes get better with age so you can even make it weeks in advance.

Rich Dark Fruitcake

Chopped pitted dates	1 1/2 cups	375 mL
Red glazed cherries, halved	1 1/2 cups	375 mL
Currants	1 1/3 cups	325 mL
Golden raisins	1 1/3 cups	325 mL
Brandy	1/2 cup	125 mL
Chopped pitted prunes	1/2 cup	125 mL
Sweet sherry	1/2 cup	125 mL
Butter (or hard margarine), softened	2/3 cup	150 mL
Dark brown sugar, packed	2/3 cup	150 mL
Large eggs	3	3
Apricot jam, warmed	1/3 cup	75 mL
Grated lemon zest	1 tbsp.	15 mL
All-purpose flour	2 cups	500 mL
Cocoa, sifted if lumpy	2 tbsp.	30 mL
Baking powder	1 tsp.	5 mL
Ground cinnamon	1 tsp.	5 mL
Ground nutmeg	1 tsp.	5 mL
Ground cloves	1/4 tsp.	1 mL
Chopped walnuts, toasted (see Tip, page 72)	1 1/2 cups	375 mL
Walnut halves	1/4 cup	60 mL
Red (or green) glazed cherries, halved	2 tbsp.	30 mL
Sweet sherry	1/4 cup	60 mL

Combine first 7 ingredients in large bowl. Let stand, covered, at room temperature for 2 days.

Cream butter and brown sugar in separate large bowl. Add eggs, 1 at a time, beating well after each addition.

Add jam and lemon zest. Stir. Mixture may look curdled.

(continued on next page)

Combine next 6 ingredients in medium bowl. Add to butter mixture
in 2 additions, mixing well after each addition until no dry flour remains.
Add chopped walnuts and fruit mixture. Stir well. Line bottom of ungreased
9 inch (22 cm) springform pan with 3 layers of parchment (not waxed) paper.
Line side with 3 layers, extending about 2 inches (5 cm) higher than side of pan.
Spread batter evenly in pan.

Arrange walnut halves and second amount of cherries around edge of batter.
Bake in 325°F (160°C) oven for 2 to 2 1/2 hours until firm and knife inserted
in centre comes out clean. Transfer pan to wire rack.

Drizzle second amount of sherry over hot cake. Cover loosely with foil.
Let stand until cooled completely. Remove cake from pan. Remove and
discard parchment paper. Wrap with plastic wrap. Wrap with foil. Let stand
in refrigerator for at least 3 days before serving. Store in airtight container
in refrigerator for up to 1 month. To serve, cut into very thin wedges.
Cuts into about 64 wedges.

1 wedge: 110 Calories; 4.3 g Total Fat (0.8 g Mono, 1.6 g Poly, 1.5 g Sat); 15 mg Cholesterol;
16 g Carbohydrate; 1 g Fibre; 2 g Protein; 23 mg Sodium

This lighter fruitcake is well worth the two weeks it takes to prepare.

Honey Jewel Cake

Glazed pineapple, chopped	1 cup	250 mL
Red (or green) glazed cherries, coarsely chopped	1 cup	250 mL
Sultana raisins	1 cup	250 mL
Golden raisins	2/3 cup	150 mL
Diced mixed peel	1/2 cup	125 mL
Medium sherry	1/4 cup	60 mL
Ground almonds	1/2 cup	125 mL
Butter, softened	1 cup	250 mL
Liquid honey	1/2 cup	125 mL
Granulated sugar	1/3 cup	75 mL
Large eggs	4	4
Grated lemon zest	2 tsp.	10 mL
Grated orange zest	2 tsp.	10 mL
All-purpose flour	1 3/4 cups	425 mL
Baking powder	1/2 tsp.	2 mL
Salt	1/4 tsp.	1 mL
Slivered almonds	1 1/2 cups	375 mL
Red (or green) glazed cherries (optional)	1/3 cup	75 mL
Whole blanched almonds (optional)	1/3 cup	75 mL
Medium sherry	3 tbsp.	50 mL
Cheesecloth		

Combine first 5 ingredients in large bowl. Drizzle with first amount of sherry. Mix well. Let stand, covered, at room temperature for at least 6 hours or overnight.

Add ground almonds. Toss until coated. Set aside.

Cream next 3 ingredients in separate large bowl. Add eggs, 1 at a time, beating well after each addition. Beat in lemon zest and orange zest.

Combine next 3 ingredients in medium bowl. Add to butter mixture in 2 additions, mixing well after each addition until no dry flour remains.

Stir in slivered almonds. Add to fruit mixture. Stir well. Spread batter in 2 greased parchment (not waxed) paper-lined 8 x 4 x 3 inch (20 x 10 x 7.5 cm) loaf pans. Bake in 300°F (150°C) oven for 40 minutes.

(continued on next page)

Arrange second amount of cherries and whole almonds over tops of loaves. Bake for another 1 1/2 to 2 hours until wooden pick inserted in centre comes out clean. Let stand in pans on wire racks until cooled completely. Remove loaves from pans. Remove and discard parchment paper.

Randomly poke several holes with skewer in top of loaves. Drizzle 1 tbsp. (15 mL) of second amount of sherry over each loaf. Put 4 layers of cheesecloth into separate medium bowl. Pour remaining sherry over top. Let stand until sherry is absorbed, adding more sherry if necessary to soak cheesecloth. Wrap loaves with cheesecloth. Wrap with waxed paper. Wrap tightly with foil. Store in refrigerator for 2 weeks. Check loaves after 1 week. Moisten cheesecloth with additional sherry if necessary. Store uncut loaves in refrigerator for up to 10 weeks. Cut loaves into 1/2 inch (12 mm) slices. Cut slices into 3 pieces each. Makes about 96 pieces.

1 piece: 66 Calories; 3.1 g Total Fat (1.1 g Mono, 0.3 g Poly, 1.3 g Sat); 14 mg Cholesterol; 9 g Carbohydrate; 1 g Fibre; 1 g Protein; 27 mg Sodium

Pictured below.

Throughout this book measurements are given in Conventional and Metric measure. To compensate for differences between the two measurements due to rounding, a full metric measure is not always used. The cup used is the standard 8 fluid ounce. Temperature is given in degrees Fahrenheit and Celsius. Baking pan measurements are in inches and centimetres as well as quarts and litres. An exact metric conversion is given on this page as well as the working equivalent (Metric Standard Measure).

Pans

Conventional – Inches	Metric – Centimetres
8 × 8 inch	20 × 20 cm
9 × 9 inch	22 × 22 cm
9 × 13 inch	22 × 33 cm
10 × 15 inch	25 × 38 cm
11 × 17 inch	28 × 43 cm
8 × 2 inch round	20 × 5 cm
9 × 2 inch round	22 × 5 cm
10 × 4 1/2 inch tube	25 × 11 cm
8 × 4 × 3 inch loaf	20 × 10 × 7.5 cm
9 × 5 × 3 inch loaf	22 × 12.5 × 7.5 cm

Oven Temperatures

Fahrenheit (°F)	Celsius (°C)	Fahrenheit (°F)	Celsius (°C)
175°	80°	350°	175°
200°	95°	375°	190°
225°	110°	400°	205°
250°	120°	425°	220°
275°	140°	450°	230°
300°	150°	475°	240°
325°	160°	500°	260°

Spoons

Conventional Measure	Metric Exact Conversion Millilitre (mL)	Metric Standard Measure Millilitre (mL)
1/8 teaspoon (tsp.)	0.6 mL	0.5 mL
1/4 teaspoon (tsp.)	1.2 mL	1 mL
1/2 teaspoon (tsp.)	2.4 mL	2 mL
1 teaspoon (tsp.)	4.7 mL	5 mL
2 teaspoons (tsp.)	9.4 mL	10 mL
1 tablespoon (tbsp.)	14.2 mL	15 mL

Cups

1/4 cup (4 tbsp.)	56.8 mL	60 mL
1/3 cup (5 1/3 tbsp.)	75.6 mL	75 mL
1/2 cup (8 tbsp.)	113.7 mL	125 mL
2/3 cup (10 2/3 tbsp.)	151.2 mL	150 mL
3/4 cup (12 tbsp.)	170.5 mL	175 mL
1 cup (16 tbsp.)	227.3 mL	250 mL
4 1/2 cups	1022.9 mL	1000 mL (1 L)

Dry Measurements

Conventional Measure Ounces (oz.)	Metric Exact Conversion Grams (g)	Metric Standard Measure Grams (g)
1 oz.	28.3 g	28 g
2 oz.	56.7 g	57 g
3 oz.	85.0 g	85 g
4 oz.	113.4 g	125 g
5 oz.	141.7 g	140 g
6 oz.	170.1 g	170 g
7 oz.	198.4 g	200 g
8 oz.	226.8 g	250 g
16 oz.	453.6 g	500 g
32 oz.	907.2 g	1000 g (1 kg)

Casseroles

Canada & Britain		United States	
Standard Size Casserole	Exact Metric Measure	Standard Size Casserole	Exact Metric Measure
1 qt. (5 cups)	1.13 L	1 qt. (4 cups)	900 mL
1 1/2 qts. (7 1/2 cups)	1.69 L	1 1/2 qts. (6 cups)	1.35 L
2 qts. (10 cups)	2.25 L	2 qts. (8 cups)	1.8 L
2 1/2 qts. (12 1/2 cups)	2.81 L	2 1/2 qts. (10 cups)	2.25 L
3 qts. (15 cups)	3.38 L	3 qts. (12 cups)	2.7 L
4 qts. (20 cups)	4.5 L	4 qts. (16 cups)	3.6 L
5 qts. (25 cups)	5.63 L	5 qts. (20 cups)	4.5 L

Tip Index

Recipe Index

most loved recipe collection